CASINO
CONFIDENTIAL

CASINO
CONFIDENTIAL

QUIRK BOOKS
PHILADELPHIA

Library of Congress Cataloging in Publication Number: 2007932326

ISBN: 978-1-59474-195-1

Printed in China

Typeset in Avenir, Periapt, and Trajan

Designed by Nicole Eagles
Art Directed by Joseph Hasenauer

Illustrations by OSBX

Distributed in North America by Chronicle Books
680 Second Street
San Francisco, CA 94107

10 9 8 7 6 5 4 3

Quirk Books
215 Church Street
Philadelphia, PA 19106
www.irreference.com
www.quirkbooks.com

Contents

Introduction

When it comes to gambling, I've seen it all (and done half of it).

I've seen every two-bit schmuck with a paycheck and a plan parade into my casino hoping to break the bank and start living the good life, only to have his hind quarters handed to him by some break-in blackjack dealer. I've watched the Wall Street guru pull out a fat wad of hundreds like it was Monopoly money and lose it all in minutes. And I've seen senior citizens grind away their kids' inheritance while plopped in front of the same tight slot machine all day, hoping to hit a jackpot that never comes.

No matter their age, credit score, or job description, I've seen them come in with surefire systems, lucky trinkets, and wishful thinking. And I've seen nearly all of them stumble out with a dazed look in their eyes after they lose it all, staggering like they just went twelve rounds with Ali. I've seen them play every possible way, use every system imaginable, and make every mistake a person could possibly make. The only difference was whether they lost enough for me to comp them a free buffet or lost enough for me to comp them a suite.

But then I've also seen those rarest of customers who manage to casually mosey into my fine establishment and turn the tables on us. They're actually able to win, and they consistently walk out of the casino with more money— sometimes a lot more money—than they came in with.

Now, everyone gets lucky; even a blind squirrel finds a nut once in a while. There have been those who make every mistake you could think of and still manage to pull off a win. Of course, those people usually come back the next day with dreams of quitting their day jobs, only to lose everything they won earlier, and then some.

I'm not here to talk about Mr. Lucky. I want to tell you about those smart players who quietly come in, win straight up, and then, just as quietly, leave. I've seen what actually works—what it is that separates the small handful of winners from the busloads of losers. And here's a little secret: Most of the winners aren't playing by the book.

I don't mean they're counting cards or cheating. I mean they aren't playing the way all those gambling books you see spilling off the bookstore shelves are telling you to play. You know, the ones written by those math nerds who step foot on a casino floor only if it's on the way to a *Star Trek* convention.

I know—I've read just about every gambling book ever written. I've studied the math, reviewed every theory, and watched them try to be applied in the real world day in and day out, down to the tiniest detail. And you know what? Those book followers still lose more than they win.

I don't deal in theories, cold equations, or statistical deviations. I deal in the real world of casino gambling, 24/7, 365 days a year (including Christmas). As the pit boss of a casino that would surely fire me if they knew I was writing this book, I am here to tell you the truth about casino gambling. Unlike other so-called experts, I'm not going to throw 300 pages of deep gaming theory at you, promising profits after you've had a few weeks to "thoroughly practice," "quietly reflect," "meditate," or whatever excuse they've cooked up to justify your continued losses. I'm going to give you a quick and dirty guide on how to win *today*. Not tomorrow, not next week, not next month—today.

I'm not here to make friends, and I'm not here to impress you with my knowledge of complex math or stun you with my computer programming prowess (because frankly I don't have much of the former and I'm definitely lacking the latter). I'm just going to tell you what I've seen that truly works. In short, I will tell you exactly what you need to do if you want to win in a casino on a regular basis. So if you want to put your losing ways behind you, forget everything you know about gambling and turn the page.

Brutal Reality Check: Every casino game is (gasp!) fixed.

Let me repeat that: Every. Single. Game.

And no, I don't mean they're using loaded dice, crooked wheels, or marked cards. I mean that every game in that casino has been run through the wringer by every bean counter, number cruncher, and math weenie the casino could think of, analyzed up, down, and sideways. They've made sure that if Joe Gambler sits and plays the game long enough, no matter how lucky he gets, the casino will soon manage to part the sucker from his money.

So no matter what game you're talking about—craps, blackjack, Elvis Presley slot machines, whatever—the casino makes sure that the odds are always, always, always in their favor. This advantage is called the house edge and ensures that the casinos will always remain in business. The math can get a bit complicated, but let me explain this neon devil in simple terms.

AS SIMPLE AS A COIN FLIP

Let's say that you and a buddy—we'll call him Lucky—are bored one day and decide to flip a quarter for cash. The rules are simple: Lucky flips the coin, and if it's heads, he pays you a dollar; if it's tails, you pay him a dollar. This is what's called a fair gamble—the odds are exactly 50-50, and you're both winning (or losing) even money.

After flipping about 10 times, the results look something like this:

Flip 1: Heads   Flip 6: Tails
Flip 2: Heads   Flip 7: Tails
Flip 3: Tails   Flip 8: Heads
Flip 4: Heads   Flip 9: Heads
Flip 5: Tails   Flip 10: Tails

Pretty exciting stuff, eh? But as you can see, after ten flips you've both ended up with exactly the same amount you started with. But you're feeling like it's your lucky day, so you decide to press on. And things do indeed change over the next ten flips:

Flip 11: Heads   Flip 16: Heads
Flip 12: Heads   Flip 17: Tails
Flip 13: Heads   Flip 18: Heads
Flip 14: Tails   Flip 19: Heads
Flip 15: Heads   Flip 20: Heads

Now things have gotten interesting. In the last set of flips, heads won 8 times and tails won only 2 times. After having settled up your wagers, you have won 6 more dollars than Lucky. The thought of "quitting while you're ahead" crosses your mind, but Lucky persuades you to keep going, so you flip for another 1,000 turns. Of course, anyone who's suffered through middle-school math knows what happens next: The law of averages works its magic on the coin so that the heads and the tails have pretty much evened themselves out, and they both come up about 500 times each. Sure, there were some interesting streaks where heads was creaming the snot out of tails, winning as much as 10 to 15 flips in a row. But of course the tide turned and Lucky's tails would go on its own little winning streak, eventually wiping out all of your gains and getting everybody back to zero. You guys decide to call it a day and try it again tomorrow, neither one of you up more than a buck or two. Unfortunately, if the casinos offered a completely fair gamble like what I've just described, they'd never make any freakin' money. How would they pay for the lights, the free alcohol, the scantily clad cocktail waitresses, or the $2.99 all-you-can-eat buffets? In a fair gamble, over the long run, everybody is left with exactly what they started out with, which means, in the end, nobody makes a dime.

WHAT THE HELL'S THE LONG RUN?

Anything can happen in the short term. If you flip a coin ten times, the law of averages (and every math nerd) says that you "should" get an equal number of heads and tails. In the short term, it's very possible to get ten heads in a row, but the more times you flip it—whether it's ten thousand, a million, or even a billion times—the closer the ratio gets to 50-50. So the long run is simply however long it takes for the math to catch up. And when you read about gambling and casinos, you'll be reading a lot about the long run, which most math nerds consider to be at least one million trials.

SO HOW DO THE CASINOS MAKE THEIR MONEY?

Now suppose you convince Lucky to play your little coin-flipping gamble again, this time for 10,000 flips straight through. Your friend agrees, but since he's doing all the work (that is, the actual coin flipping), he proposes a change to the usual payouts. This time, if the coin lands on tails, you'll pay him a dollar, but if it lands on heads, he'll pay you only 95 cents, reduced by a sort of cost of doing business. By charging you five cents out of every dollar, he's given himself a 5 percent advantage—a 5 percent house edge. You're not going to sweat 5 cents, so you agree, and over the course of a few flips, everything looks pretty rosy. After 20 flips, you had a nice winning streak and are up a few bucks. After 100 flips, you're up 20 bucks. After the first thousand flips, the money's started to even out, and finally after all 10,000 flips, you ended up with an exactly equal number of heads and tails—5,000 each. Now this is a sorry spectacle—not because you've spent your entire afternoon flipping a coin for cash, but because you paid Lucky $5,000 while he only had to pay you $4,750. That 5 percent house edge didn't affect you much at first, but it slowly chipped away at your winnings.

This is the biggest way that casinos guarantee they make money no matter what happens. Instead of giving you a perfectly fair gamble, they tilt the odds for every single game in their favor so that, in the long run, they will always end up ahead.

To use the easiest illustration, consider roulette. There are 36 numbers on an American roulette wheel as well as two green slots, 0 and 00, for a total of 38 possible winning numbers. So if you're placing a dollar bet on a single number such as 17, the odds of it hitting that one number are 37 to 1, because there are 37 other numbers that can hit besides the one that you bet. All's good until you realize that when 17 does in fact hit, instead of paying you $37—a fair gamble with the 37 to 1 true odds—the casino is going to give you only $35 for your $1 bet, or 35 to 1. You are losing $2 for every winning bet you make, and when you divide $2 by 38, you're losing 5.3 cents for every dollar you bet. That's why the house edge on roulette is 5.3 percent.

WHY THE HOUSE EDGE IS A GOOD THING

Now you might be thinking that the casinos are completely ripping you off by not paying true odds on your wagers. But think of the house edge as a sort of "entertainment tax," or simply the profit margin for the service provided. You don't get mad because restaurants charge more for their food than it cost them to buy and make it, do you? The casinos provide a ritzy-glitzy atmosphere with free drinks, flashing neon lights, and reasonably priced food, and they pay for these amenities by charging a sort of commission on all of your winning bets. If there were no house edge, there would be no well-regulated place to enjoy a good gamble.

HOW THE CASINO WINS EVEN WHEN YOU DO

To get back to our coin-flipping illustration, let's say your friend Lucky enjoyed his little gambling game with you so much (how could he not? He made an easy $250 for flipping a freakin' coin!) that he decided to expand his operation. Instead of just playing with you, he's invited 10,000 people to take a wager on a coin flip. He's still collecting $1 if it's heads and still paying 95 cents if it's tails. Each person gambles for about 100 flips before they decide to quit. With such a short number of flips, you get some winners and some losers, as well as some really big winners and some really big losers.

After flipping that coin a million times for 10,000 different customers, Lucky finds that there again has been an almost equal number of heads and tails, netting him a total profit of $50,000. Sure, there were times when he went on a real bad streak and was down a lot of money, but he knew for certain that if he just kept flipping that coin long enough to put the odds just in his favor—over the long run—he was guaranteed to make money.

It's the same with the casinos. Sure, there are people who come in and get lucky, make a killing, and then leave. But there are plenty who go in and lose, sometimes a lot. Given enough people and enough time, the odds are always in favor of the house. And in the end, the house always wins.

THE CATCH
(THERE'S ALWAYS A CATCH)

For nearly every game in the casino, the house edge appears to be very low. Every book and Web site on gambling will reel off the house edge numbers for each game in a chart that looks something like this:

Portion of Every Dollar Gambled That Is Kept by the Casino*

Casino Game	House Edge
Blackjack	1-2 cents
Craps	1-2 cents
Roulette	5 cents
Baccarat	1-2 cents
Pai Gow Poker	Almost 3 cents
Let It Ride	3 cents
Three-Card Poker	5 cents
Slot Machines	3-15 cents
Video Poker	1-15 cents

*Note that these numbers vary from casino to casino. They also assume that the player is using optimal strategy (and not making stupid bets).

At first glance, this chart appears to be fairly straightforward: On let it ride, for example, they're making three and a half cents on every dollar wagered over a million hands.

Naturally, then, you'd assume then that if you looked at the casino's bank statement over a year's time, you'd see that their profit margin on blackjack was about 1.5 percent, roulette was about 5 percent, and baccarat was just over 1 percent.

But you'd be completely wrong!

In fact, if their profit margin on blackjack was only 2 percent, or even 5 percent, the casino would be in serious trouble and there would be lots of people looking for other jobs.

THE HOLD

A casino's profit on a particular game is called the hold, because it's how much of the money customers gambled that the casino was able to "hold" onto. It's what the casino "won" from their customers. When casinos talk about profits and money, the discussion revolves around that all-important hold.

To put it simply, suppose someone comes up to a blackjack table and buys in for $1,000. He plays for several hours and eventually walks away with only $800. The drop, or how much money was "dropped" into the hole at the blackjack table, for that particular session was $1,000. The customer lost $200, so the casino won $200. The hold for that session was 20 percent. When you look at the average hold for table games, you'll be shocked at how much money the casinos are raking in, month in and month out.

These numbers are just averages. At a blackjack table, for example, the hold can be as low as 10 percent or as high as 22 percent. But if any game dips below 10 percent for any period, something isn't right. In 1983, the Las Vegas Hilton fired 37 longtime dealers because the shift they all worked on had some serious hold issues, and management just assumed there was cheating or collusion or something seedy going on.

Game	House Edge	Typical Hold
Blackjack	0.7%	15%
Baccarat	1.06%	10%
Craps	1.4%	20%
Roulette	5.26%	25%
Pai-Gow Poker	2.73%	15%
Three-Card Poker	5.32%	25%
Let It Ride	3.51%	25%
Slot Machines	5-10%	5-10%
Video Poker	3-8%	3-8%

Slot and video poker machines hold percentages vary wildly from machine to machine and from casino to casino. To learn how and why, see chapters 11 and 12.

In other words, if the casino's hold isn't up to par, meetings will be held, interviews will be conducted, and investigations will be carried out.

 ## HOW THE CASINOS GET YOU TO LOSE EVEN MORE

With such a huge gap between how much a game is supposed to make (thanks to the house edge) and how much it actually does make (after looking at the hold), you can't help but wonder: How, exactly, is the casino making so much more money? No, they aren't out-and-out cheating; there's too much danger of losing their license if they rip you off. But there are plenty of totally legal ways that they can get you to stop paying attention to your bet.

FREE BOOZE

Alcohol is a casino's best friend; it makes you do things no sane, rational person would ever think of doing, like betting your entire paycheck on red 22 . . .

again! In gambling terms, a fish is an easy mark, and there's a reason they try to make you drink like one.

HALF-NAKED WOMEN

Not only will casinos gladly offer you all the vodka tonics you can handle, they'll have lingerie models posing as cocktail waitresses to pour the beverages down your gullet. The casino is more than happy to keep you drinking and mindlessly gambling, and the waitresses know that big drinkers mean bigger tips.

PRETTY LIGHTS

Casinos burn through enough electricity in a day to power most third-world countries. The flashing neon lights and the blinking slot machines are enough to dazzle most visitors into a state of delirium. Casinos spend millions of dollars studying human psychology and what motivates us to take risks. That's why you see so much red, especially on slot machines—the color supposedly attracts players and gets them to think victory. They set the lighting bright enough so that a player can see what's going on but not so bright that it is mentally draining. They've even experimented with different scents as a sort of gamblers' aromatherapy, in the hope that the smell of wormwood would cause you to uncontrollably withdraw money from the ATM.

PUMPING OXYGEN INTO THE CASINO

Baloney! This is just an urban legend. What possible reason could a smoke-filled casino have to siphon in oxygen to guests? That'd only make them happier, light-headed, and perhaps a bit more willing to spend money they can't afford to lose. And who really wants that?

NO CLOCKS

If you ever go to a casino without a watch, good luck finding out what time it is. The only clocks are on the employees' timecards. Casinos want you to lose track of time; that's why windows are so rare. Walk into a casino and there's only one time. It could be five in the afternoon or five in the morning, but in the casino it's always forget-your-troubles time.

COMPLIMENTARIES

Not only are drinks served free, but if you're the type of customer casinos are looking for (that is, one willing to lose lots of money), we'll even give you free food. Look on the bright side, if you visit and lose a month's pay, at least you got comped a free buffet, right? And if you happen to win a month's pay, we're definitely going to do whatever we can to keep you there so you'll play again and we can win it back. If you're a big winner, we're your best friend. Want a nice complimentary dinner for two? A hotel room? Perhaps a free bottle of bubbly? Absolutely no problem. We want you to think to yourself, "Wow, these guys are great! I don't want to leave just yet; why don't we stay another day or two and play some more? After all, we're still playing with 'their' money."

CHIPS INSTEAD OF CASH

Whoever invented chips was a genius. Plopping down a stack of $100 black chips isn't as painful as plopping down a stack of $100 bills. Even though you know in your head it's the same thing, it's ever so slightly easier to push out those chips.

Whenever you win a small jackpot at the tables, instead of giving you the choice of paying you in cash or chips, dealers automatically pay you in chips. Cash goes straight into your pocket, and the casino might never see it again. But if we pay you in chips, hopefully you'll just set your winnings next to your other stacks and burn right through them without a second thought.

Have you ever noticed that there are a dozen places in a casino to buy chips—blackjack, craps, pai gow—but there's only one place you can cash them out? That's right, the cashier cage . . . located in the middle of the entire casino . . . and there's only one window open . . . and you have to wait in a huge line that marches right past all those glorious slot machines.

RAT MAZES

Sure, those humongo casinos on the Las Vegas strip get all the press, but it's the smaller casinos with the cramped, maze-like floors jammed with machines that get all the money. Tourists want to be dazzled, but real players want intimacy. They want lots of slot machines crammed into smaller private areas. That's why casinos are built like labyrinths, and visitors must navigate bank after bank of wonderfully profitable slot machines before you can actually get anywhere, be it the cashier, your hotel room, or, God forbid, the exit.

PLAYER'S CLUBS

We'd love for you to join the Player's Club. That way, we can reward you with things like cash back on your slot play or maybe a free meal now and then. Of course, we can now keep detailed records of which machines you play, when you play them, and how much money you spend down to the dollar—but that has nothing to do with it. And just because we now have your address and date of birth doesn't mean we'll necessarily flood your mailbox with targeted offers for the holidays and your birthday—but we probably will.

GOOD OLD-FASHIONED GREED

None of the elements listed above compare to plain, simple greed. When a player is winning, no matter how much, he wants to win more, so he keeps playing. And more often than not, he plays until he loses it all. Then he pulls out even more money, thinking, "If I did it once, I can do it again," only to lose that money too. But now we've got our hooks in him, and he'll always remember that one time when he was killing the casino for thousands, and he'll keep coming back hoping to repeat. Thank God for greed, or I'd be out of a job. Most people wouldn't even come into a casino, but hey! Have you heard? We're giving away free cars, free trips, free money! You'd be a fool not to come on down this weekend! We can barely stay in business with all the money we're just giving away!

CHAPTER 2

Gambling is a lot like driving: Everyone thinks they somehow have a natural talent that makes them the best driver on the road, when really it's a wonder they ever make it to work alive.

I can never understand it: People who pick up the game of golf will read numerous golf articles or ask others for advice; chess players will study books on the game; and football players train, train, train to become the absolute best they can possibly be. But when it comes to gambling, the closest thing people have to a plan is deciding whether they're going to withdraw $100 from their checking account or from their savings account.

I know gambling ain't an Olympic sport, but sheesh, even kids playing Candy Land have some kind of strategy. Most gamblers simply go to the closest casino, pick the first slot

The Five Keys to Successful Gambling

machine or blackjack table they come to, and bet whatever their "gut" tells them. Sure, their gut hasn't done too well when it comes to picking winning lottery numbers, future spouses, or even which checkout line to get in, but why shouldn't it work at a game of chance that they barely understand?

It doesn't help that most gambling books encourage the strategy of playing only what you can afford to lose, blinding you with page upon page of mind-numbing statistics that all boil down to the belief that, in the long run, you'll never win. They've already built it into your head that you are going to lose; they're just going to show you how to lose less than your average casino schmuck. But listen to me: I have seen plenty of winning players, and while some of them were just plain lucky, others were able to win consistently. They all share common traits, which you must make a part of your casino arsenal.

Sounds like work? Of course it is. If you're afraid of a little sweat and study, keep playing the way you're playing. It's people like you who ensure my continued employment, so why should I try to stop you? But if you want to actually improve your chances of going home a winner, you must know the Five Keys to Successful Gambling.

① KNOWLEDGE

I'll never forget one loser who ran up to one of my tables, burned through $100 on various bets, and then ten minutes into it asked me, "What's the name of this game again?" Trying to keep from laughing, I replied, "Uh, it's roulette."

Why is it that people won't trust a certified public accountant without a background check but don't have a problem throwing their money at a casino game that they don't even know the rules to?

If you want to make any money at the casino, you absolutely need to know the games you are playing—*before* you enter the casino. I'm not saying you need to study them like you are writing a doctoral thesis, but at least know how it is played. Pick up a book (like this one). Learn the rules of the game. And decide upon a strategy.

COMPUTERIZED TRAINING

Personal computers do everything these days: They let you book your airline travel, do your own taxes, meet beautiful and mysterious eastern European women who will marry you for the price of airfare. But computers also help average gamblers become smart gamblers. Before they ever step foot into a casino, smart gamblers will have practiced a game hundreds of times using computer simulations. With the right software (there are dozens of choices on the market), you can study exactly how a game is played—with no pressure from the person next to you to hurry it up. And there will be no flashing lights or ringing bells to distract you, either. You'll have time to focus and to ponder the various rules for each game, from craps to roulette. And you can experiment with numerous gambling methods to see how they work in actual test runs instead of just on paper.

 RULE CHANGES

Of course, computers can teach you only so much. It's not enough to simply know how a game is played. You need to be aware of how "house rules" vary from one casino to the next. In blackjack, for instance, some casinos will only let you double on 10 or 11; others let you double on any first two cards. In craps, you can sometimes get 10 times for your odds bets, while other casinos will only let you take 3 times odds. Once you learn what these things mean, research different casinos to see who offers what—and shop around for the best gamble.

2 BANKROLL

The problem with nine out of ten players is that they come to the casino with only a few dollars and a dream, hoping to turn a sawbuck into a life-changing jackpot. Twenty minutes later, they're broke and heading to the ATM.

I see people sit down at a $10 table and buy in for $100. What are they thinking? Ten hands! That's all they have money for if things go bad, which they usually do.

Of course, a hundred bucks isn't exactly chump change either, which is why most people think $100 is plenty to play with. It is—if you're playing at the $1 tables.

Most people's bankroll is closer to Donald Duck's than Donald Trump's (mine included), but that's okay. In the real world, people have wives and ex-wives and car payments and mortgage payments and childcare bills and doctor bills and on and on, so $100 is a lot of money. But you've got to be realistic: If you've got only $100 or $200 to play with, you shouldn't be sitting down at the $25 tables, because:

{ SMALL BANKROLL = SCARED MONEY }

If you sit down at a $25 table with $200, you've got enough for eight bets if you lose every one. So what happens if you lose the first two? Now, a quarter of your bankroll's already been wiped out and you've only been there for two minutes. Do you think you're going to be able to play the way you're supposed to? Are you going to double down against a dealer's Ten even though billions of computer simulations say that is exactly what you're supposed to do? Absolutely, positively not.

So when you come to the casino to play any table game, if you want to relax and not sweat the money, you should have a bankroll of 100 times your smallest bet.

Yes, you heard right:

{ YOUR BANKROLL SHOULD BE 100 TIMES YOUR SMALLEST BET }

It doesn't matter if you're playing blackjack, Texas hold 'em, or craps, you should not come to the casino unless you have 100 times your smallest bet. So if you are going to come to the casino with $100, you should limit your action to the $1 tables. If you want to play the $5 tables, bring $500.

Games like blackjack and craps can be brutal, with fast swings. The more money you have to play with, the more you can sweat the bad bets and losing streaks. The more money you have, the easier it is to be disciplined and play within your predetermined strategy without getting cold feet. You're not going to start cursing and playing scared if you've got the bankroll to back it up.

I've seen it a million times: Your $100 buy-in is rapidly getting sucked away, and before you know it, you're down to your last 30 bucks at a $10 table and playing stupid, quickly losing it all. Now, what do you think your car ride home is going to be like? How's the rest of your evening going to be? Terrible! All this could've been avoided if you'd simply followed my bankroll advice.

Now you're all screaming, "A hundred times the smallest bet? A hundred times the smallest bet! But I'm used to playing at $25 tables! That means I have to start with $2,500!" Well, if you were winning at those $25 tables, you wouldn't be reading this book, would you? You may like the feeling of being a $25 green-chip player, Mr. Big-Shot High Roller, but you'll be considered more of a big shot if you actually win at the table instead of blowing through your entire wad before the cocktail waitress can even bring you a drink.

How are you supposed to save that kind of money? Well, just set aside the little bit you would have used for your next trip and then don't go. Do that three or four times, and before you know it, you'll have your minimum bankroll. I know, I know, easier said than done. But if you want to win at the casinos, you need some discipline. Having fun is for tourists.

3 GAME PLAN

You need a game plan long before you get to the casino. Does any Super Bowl team go into the game with just a few rough ideas of what they're going to do, and then draw up plays in the huddle? Make no mistake, this is war: you versus the casino. The casino has thought of everything: They know exactly what they'll do in absolutely every single situation you present. They've planned everything from the lighting down to the gaudy-awful carpeting. They have no qualms about taking every single penny you have, and they've perfected every single method they're going to use to do so.

So why would you just mosey up to any old table and plunk down whatever you might have in your wallet? The casino has you outgunned on every front. They've manipulated every game so they always have the advantage. They have a nearly unlimited bankroll. They can handle whatever action you throw their way. They never grow tired and never need a rest. And you think you have a chance going in and flying by the seat of your pants? Do you think you have some innate ability to win thousands when the millions of people before you have lost billions? Give me a break.

In each of the chapters that follow, I will show you a plan of attack for the most popular games in any casino. I will show you how to find profitable situations. I'll show you how to spot good casinos, good games, and good dealers.

I will show you what works and what doesn't, so you can go in prepared.

4 TRENDS

Every time you step into a casino, you're hoping to "get lucky" or catch a "good run" of cards, because otherwise the ever-present house edge will doom you to bankruptcy. The math nerds insist again and again that no amount of finagling can overcome the house edge, and that you'll always lose in the long run. They'll tell you that you'll lose two cents for every dollar bet in blackjack, period. But anyone who's ever doubled down on an 11 knows that there are winners all the time—otherwise we'd never come back.

"Sure," the math weenies say, "there are winners, but that's nothing more than standard deviation and random variance." This is a fancy way of saying that anyone can sometimes go on a winning streak. "If you continue to play, you'll eventually lose all your money. And we have the billions of computer-simulated tests proving just that fact."

News flash: We're never going to play a billion hands of blackjack or even see a million rolls of the dice. We'll never give that slot-machine handle ten million pulls, so we'll never, ever experience the long run that the math weenies are always talking about.

No matter what we play, we're going to experience some trend one way or another: We'll have a losing streak, a winning streak, or simply break even.

I've seen players employ every kind of superstition—rubbing a rabbit's foot, making the sign of a cross, kissing photographs of their children, and so on. Sometimes they work, other times they don't. When you step into a casino, everything you need to know about luck boils down to good trends and bad trends. And the only way you're ever going to win at a casino is to find and then exploit good trends when they come along. But you also need to be able to identify losing trends so you can cut your losses and get out of Dodge.

Remember: Trends are your friends. In the chapters to come, I'll tell you how to identify tables and slot machines that are likely to produce winning streaks—good trends. I'll also show the warning signs of bad trends so you'll know how to avoid them.

5 MONEY MANAGEMENT

Once you've found a hot trend, how do you go about exploiting it? That's where money management comes in. And I'm not talking about balancing your checkbook. I'm talking about how much you bet and how you bet it. The math weenies say that it doesn't matter how you bet . . . in the long run. But that's just stupid. Of course it matters how you bet. Most people play by their gut. And when you consider that new casinos are sprouting up all over the country, it's clear the gut doesn't have a clue.

TYPES OF BETS

Ever since Og bet Grog that he could make fire, humankind has been looking for systems that would overcome the house edge. Most of them are simple betting progressions.

In a nutshell, there are only three types of betting:

- **Flat Betting:** This is merely betting the same amount every single time. For example, if you're at a $5 table, you might decide to bet one unit, or $5, and stick with it, win or lose.
- **Negative Progression:** This is an "up as you lose" method of betting that sees you raising your bets each time you lose, hoping to recoup some or all of your previous losses. This type is financial suicide and will destroy your bankroll in addition to your sanity. I talk more about these systems in chapter 13.
- **Positive Progression:** This is an "up as you win" style of betting. Instead of betting more when you lose, you bet more only when you win, taking advantage of a winning trend. This is, without question, the best way to bet. Each table game is unique, so betting should be approached slightly differently for each. The chapters for each game discuss in detail how and when to bet.

THE NEW YORK PROGRESSION

The absolute best positive progression method I know and use is called the New York progression, so named because of the New York City area code 212. Start by betting two units as your base bet, each unit being whatever you decided was your absolute minimum bet. So if you're at a $5 minimum table, your first bet would be $10. If you win, you lock up some money by lowering your next bet to one unit, or $5. That way you're guaranteed a profit. If you win that bet as well, you take it back up to $10 in hopes of catching a winning streak and then continue with the following progression: 2, 1, 2, 3, 4, 5, 6, and so on. If you lose any bet, you return or continue your base bet of two units.

A sample progression would be:

Outcome	Next Bet	Running Profits
Initial Bet	$10	$0
Win	$5	$10
Win	$10	$15
Win	$15	$25
Win	$20	$40
Lose	$10	$30
Lose	$10	$20
Win	$5	$25

BE REASONABLE WITH YOUR WIN GOALS

Too many times I see people march into the casino with dollar signs in their eyes, hoping to make the ultimate score so they can retire and see the world. But you need to be realistic. You aren't going to break the bank.

Some ultraconservatives say that getting a 20 percent return on your gambling dollar is ideal. While that may be wonderful in the stock market, I figure you came here to gamble, not to grind out lunch money. Though you should realize that you aren't going to walk away wealthy, don't limit yourself to winning spare change, either. If the cards go your way, you want to get at least a 50 percent return on your money.

Say you started with a bankroll of $1,000 at blackjack and decided to play the $10 tables. After following my positive progression method (outlined in chapter 3) for a few hours, lo and behold, you're up $500. A lot of people wouldn't be happy with a 50 percent return on their money. They want to triple or quadruple it.

Time and time again I've seen people winning but just not being satisfied with however much they had. They go on huge runs and make tons of money, but the cards inevitably turn and they give it all back—all the winnings and their original bankroll, too. They can't shake the feeling that "If I did it once, I can do it again." That, my friends, is how the casinos stay in business.

Once you hit the 50 percent mark, be prepared to stop at any moment. And I don't mean stop to go for a smoke break—I mean stop for the day. You've already gotten a 50 percent return; how much more do you want?

These should be your goals:

1. **Win 50 times your minimum bet** (or win 50 percent of your bankroll).

2. **If you've won 50 times your minimum bet,** be prepared to beat a hasty retreat, but never quit when you're winning. As long as you haven't lost three in a row, keep playing. Who knows—maybe you'll catch another streak.

3. **If you lose three in a row,** get up from the table, but don't go to another table. Go home, or go back to your room, or go out to dinner. Just end your gambling session now. Enjoy your winnings! Go buy something nice with it or just gloat over your luck.

4. **If you go back and forth with the dealer,** winning a few hands and losing a few hands, stop when you lose 20 percent of your profits. So if you've won $500 in profit, absolutely do not continue to play if you've given back $100. This way you've allowed time to see if things would turn back around, but you haven't given back your winnings.

BE REASONABLE WITH YOUR LOSSES

Most people's idea of stop losses is to merely play until they're out of money. But you need to be smarter.

This is going to be painful for many to hear, but you need to quit when you lose half of your bankroll. Yes, you heard that right. Not when you lose all of your bankroll, not when you've maxed out your credit cards, and not when you hit the daily limit at the ATM. You need to leave when you've lost half the money you brought to play with for that session.

Why? Very simple: The feeling of having lost everything is pretty tough. If you stumble out of the casino without enough cash to tip the valet, then you're going to feel miserable for the rest of the week. Who knows? You might even swear off gambling for good, and we know you don't want to do that.

On the other hand, if you lose money but still go home with a reasonable amount of cash in your pocket, you'll have lost the battle but not the war.

CHAPTER 3

Nowadays, you can go from Venice to Vegas, and every Podunk casino in between, and find blackjack tables packed with desperate players. But there was a time when the game of 21 was anything but popular. Back in the 1930s and '40s, casinos had only one or two blackjack tables, and they were always stuck way in the back, empty.

Then along came good ol' MIT professor Edward O. Thorp, math nerd extraordinaire.

In 1962, Thorp published *Beat the Dealer*, a book that actually showed how a player could beat blackjack. Using fancy computers, Thorp not only figured out the best strategy for each and every hand but also invented the first card-counting system, and pit bosses haven't slept soundly since.

Once everyone found out that it was indeed possible to win at a casino, people rushed the blackjack tables, even if most didn't know a blackjack shoe from Shinola. Sure, the casinos loved all the action at first—until they learned about Professor Thorp and his little book. They were so scared that they changed all the rules to kill the counter—and killed all their business in the process. The casinos eventually relented—sorta. They gave back enough of the game to bring in the customers, but kept enough rule changes to keep counters away. Nevertheless, the belief persists that blackjack is winnable if you just know what you're doing.

BLACKJACK TABLE

DEALER MUST DRAW TO 16 & STAND ON ALL 17'S

INSURANCE PAYS 2 TO 1

HOW THE GAME IS PLAYED

Playing blackjack is easy. The hardest part is being able to count to 21, which most gamblers can handle (even if they have to use all their fingers and toes).

Despite what most beginners think, your goal isn't to get as close as you can to 21. Your goal is simply to have a higher total than the dealer without "busting," or going over 21.

Blackjack is played with a standard 52-card deck (no jokers), but all face cards count as 10. So if you have a Ten card and a Jack and the dealer has a King and a Queen, both of your hands equal exactly 20. An Ace counts as either 1 or 11, whichever is better for your hand. So if you have two Fives and an Ace, they add up to 21 instead of 11. But if you have a Five and a Six and then draw an Ace, you'll have 12 instead of a busting 22. An Ace that gives you two nonbusting totals is "soft"—for example, a Seven with an Ace is a soft 18, because the hand could total either 8 or 18; a face card with an Eight would make a hard 18.

SOFT HAND   HARD HAND   BLACKJACK

In the most popular form of the game, the dealer gives you two cards face up and also gives himself two cards—one face up, the other face down (the hidden card is called the dealer's hole card).

 ## A TYPICAL HAND

Let's take you through an actual blackjack hand to show you how it's done. You enter the casino and go to a table with a sign that says $5–$500, which are your minimum and maximum betting limits. You take a seat and set a $100 bill on the table (at most casinos, dealers aren't allowed to take anything directly from your hand to curb cheating). She gives you chips, you place $10 worth in the betting circle, and the round begins. The dealer deals you a Five card and a Four card (for a total of 9) while she shows a Seven. A 9 is pretty small, and since there's no possibility of busting no matter what card you take next, you go ahead and scrape your forefinger toward you to signal "hit me." The dealer gives you a Queen, making a grand total of 19. This is a pretty good hand, so you wave over your bet, signaling you want to stand, or stay.

The dealer has certain rules that she has to follow no matter what, but you're free to do whatever you want. When the dealer turns over her other card, she has to follow the rules set by the casino, which means she takes a card (or hit) anytime her cards add up to 16 or less. At some casinos, she stands on all totals of 17, while others make her hit if she's got a soft 17, such as an Ace-Six or Three-Three-Ace. She must stop when she has a total of at least 17 no matter what; you, on the other hand, can play however you want, regardless of your total.

So now the dealer flips over her hole card to reveal a Jack, which gives her a total of 17. Even though she can see that you have 19, clearly higher than her 17, house rules force her to stay. She slides your winnings next to your original bet, then scoops up the cards and gets ready to deal another hand.

HOW THE HOUSE GETS ITS EDGE

Sure, it looks like it's an even match against the dealer, especially since you get to make all the decisions and she's stuck following the exact same strategy every single time. But because you have to act first, while the dealer waits until everyone else is done, she gets the advantage: You'll bust first and lose, regardless of whether or not the dealer would have busted.

 INSURANCE

Let's play another pretend hand. In this one, you're dealt a pair of Tens while the dealer shows an Ace. If the dealer has a blackjack, everyone at the table automatically loses their money, unless another person also has a blackjack (in which case, it's a push, or a draw, and the bet is neither won nor lost). But before the dealer checks her hole card, she asks if you'd like to buy "insurance." Here you have the chance to place a side bet that she has a blackjack, by betting up to half your original bet. If you place the insurance bet and she does have a blackjack, you lose your original bet but still get paid 2 to 1 on your insurance bet, so you end up with what you started with. But that's only if she has a blackjack. If she doesn't, you lose your insurance bet, and play resumes. Unfortunately, all side bets are sucker bets, and insurance is no exception. The dealer will have a blackjack less than one third of the time. You should almost never, ever take insurance, whether you have 12 or 20.

However, when you have a blackjack and the dealer shows an Ace up, she'll offer you even money before she checks for a blackjack (which would be a push). If you take her offer, she'll pay you even money instead of the usual 3 to 2, whether she ends up with a blackjack or not. The odds are still the same that she doesn't, but I'm telling you to take even money. Psychologically, it's much better to win something when you finally get a blackjack than when you just get a push. I know, I know, mathematically, in the long run, you won't make as much money, but I say better a bird in the hand (now) than two in the bush (tomorrow).

SPLITTING AND DOUBLING

The house almost always has you over a barrel when you play blackjack, but you can do some things the dealer can't. Not only do you get paid 3 to 2 on a blackjack (the dealer only makes even money), you can also do what's called splitting and doubling. Since in the long run you win only 44 hands out of 100 while the dealer wins 48 (the other eight hands are pushes), this is where most of the money you can make at blackjack comes from. If you couldn't split or double, blackjack would be one of the worst bets in the casino.

DOUBLING

Whenever your card totals tell you you're more likely to win and the dealer is more likely to lose, you want to double. You get to increase the size of your bet by any amount up to twice your original bet, but in exchange for doing so, you get only one card. That's okay because the odds tell you you're going to win enough times to make it worthwhile in the long run.

SPLITTING

Another basic blackjack rule is the ability to split pairs. If you're dealt a pair of Eights on your $10 bet, you can choose to throw up another $10 to split them, essentially creating two hands of 8 each. But unlike doubling, you can take as many cards as you want on either hand and hopefully win twice as much. However, just because you can split a pair doesn't mean you should. Some pairs you should never split, and others you should split only when the dealer has a certain card up. I'll tell you how to recognize good splits later in this chapter.

PLAN OF ATTACK

The math nerds would have us believe that there is no way, no how that black-jack can be beaten without counting cards, and they use billions of computer-simulated hands of blackjack to prove it. Sure, they say, you may experience a little random variation now and then (that is, a winning streak), but in the long run, you're going to lose two cents of every dollar bet.

So how have I personally watched what feels like billions of actual, real live hands of blackjack and seen people win, sometimes more than the odds say they should? The key is to do all you can to increase your chances of experiencing that random variation a bit beyond what simple chance would allow.

LEARN AND PLAY BASIC STRATEGY RELIGIOUSLY

There was a time when things like "strategy," "plans," or "general concept of what the hell I'm doing" weren't big buzzwords among blackjack players. But today, people with far more brains, far more computing power, and far more free time than you or I will ever enjoy have analyzed every angle and every possible combination to calculate the best moves for blackjack. The fruits of their Pentiums have given the world "basic strategy," a relatively simple chart that shows in graphic detail how you should play each and every hand.

Now, I know I've pooh-poohed many a math nerd who can't see beyond his perfectly calculated world, but I've also seen basic strategy applied (and more often ignored) in any number of casinos, every single day. Casinos love people who ignore basic strategy because they know they'll eventually get all these people's money. In short, there is no way you can expect to win more than a session or two if you don't religiously follow basic strategy.

Are you guaranteed to win with basic strategy? Of course not. Only solid money-management techniques can guarantee consistent winning. But if you don't use basic strategy, you might as well not even go to the casino—just write out a check for how much you planned on spending and send it to the owners. That way, you cut out the middleman.

DIFFERENT GAMES, DIFFERENT CHARTS

There are strategy charts for every possible rule variation you'll ever encounter at a casino, and they all promise to boost your winnings over basic strategy by as much as a whole one-tenth of a percent! But you could drive yourself nuts memorizing every rule change and the appropriate strategy. For a tenth of a penny, it's just not worth it.

You're better off memorizing this one chart and applying it to every regular blackjack game you encounter, whether single deck or multideck.

The chart on pages 40–41 tells you how to handle each and every hand you get in blackjack. You simply look at your card total—whether you have two, three or more cards, or even a split—and line it up with the dealer's up card to find out what action to take. So if you split a pair of Eights (which the chart says you should always do), and hit the first Eight and got a Three, reconsult the chart to see that you should double your 11 against any dealer up card except an Ace.

It may be confusing at first, but when you practice at home, you'll see that most basic-strategy decisions make sense. If you have problems memorizing charts, simply take it with you. Most casinos don't have a problem with you consulting a basic-strategy chart (some casino gift shops even sell them).

One last thing: A few casinos allow players to "surrender" half their bet when they're in a near no-win situation. Unlike most casino offerings, this is actually a good thing, as long as you stick with the chart.

THE MOST COMMON BASIC STRATEGY MISTAKES

- **Playing bonuses.** Remember, side bets are sucker bets. No matter how good it sounds or seems, trust me: They wouldn't be there unless the casino made a ton of money off them.
- **Splitting Tens.** Why would you want to take a near-perfect, almost-

THE ONLY BASIC STRATEGY CHART
YOU'LL EVER NEED

PLAYER'S HAND	2	3	4	5	6	7	8	9	10	A
A - A	SP	SP	SP	SP	SP	SP	SP	SP	SP	SP
10 - 10										
9 - 9	SP	SP	SP	SP	SP		SP	SP		
8 - 8	SP	SP	SP	SP	SP	SP	SP	SP	SP	SP
7 - 7	SP	SP	SP	SP	SP	SP				
6 - 6		SP	SP	SP	SP					
5 - 5	DD	DD	DD	DD	DD	DD	DD	DD		
4 - 4										
3 - 3			SP	SP	SP	SP				
2 - 2			SP	SP	SP	SP				

DEALER'S UPCARD

STAND ☐

DD double down
if you can't, stand

split SP

HIT ☐

DD double down
if you can't, hit

SR surrender
if you can't, hit

PLAYER'S HAND	2	3	4	5	6	7	8	9	10	A
SOFT 19-21										
SOFT 18		DD	DD	DD	DD					
SOFT 17		DD	DD	DD	DD					
SOFT 16			DD	DD	DD					
SOFT 15			DD	DD	DD					
SOFT 14				DD	DD					
SOFT 13				DD	DD					
HARD 17-21										
HARD 16								SR	SR	SR
HARD 15									SR	
HARD 14										
HARD 13										
HARD 12										
11	DD	DD	DD	DD	DD	DD	DD	DD	DD	
10	DD	DD	DD	DD	DD	DD	DD	DD		
9		DD	DD	DD	DD	DD				
8										
7										
6										
5										

UPCARD

guaranteed-winning hand and muck it up? What are you hoping for? To get another Ten? Are you going to split that one, too? Never, never, never!

- **Splitting just because you can.** For some reason, people think that just because they have a pair, they have to split them, even if it's a pair of Twos against my Queen. Congratulations! You've just turned one crappy hand into two crappy hands!

- **Not doubling when you should.** People hate to double against any high card, even if billions of computer simulations, mathematicians, and the world's greatest gambling minds say otherwise. But hey, maybe you know something they don't.

- **Standing on a 16.** You pray that the dealer will deal himself 16, knowing it's the absolute worst hand to have, but when you finally get one, you panic and won't take a card, even if he has a Ten card showing. Face it: The odds are you're going to lose this hand anyway, so you're better off going down swinging, with the chance of hitting a good card, than counting on the dealer busting.

A QUICK WORD ON CARD COUNTING

Despite what books, movies, and TV would have you believe, card counting is hard, hard, hard. It's not something Joe Average could master in an evening or even a week.

The infamous MIT team proved that card counting works—with a heavy emphasis on "work." First you have to spend numerous hours in practice, practice, practice counting down multiple decks. Then you have to find those few casinos that might have an exploitable game. Then you have to look like you're a clueless tourist while you perform fairly advanced math, all the while hiding the fact that you do know what the hell you're doing. And do you know how much you're supposed to make at most?

Two cents for every dollar!

That's it! Even if you can master the most sophisticated and complicated card-counting systems ever devised, your advantage is—in the most perfect of circumstances—only 2 percent. True, the MIT team made a bit of money, but they had to bet millions of dollars to see any kind of decent return, and they suffered through some brutal losing streaks.

After all I've seen, I really think that if you want to count cards, you do it for the intellectual challenge and not because you think you can get rich. Even Professor Thorp didn't make his fortune playing blackjack (he got rich in the stock market). If you're willing to put in that much effort, there are better and easier ways to win at blackjack.

THE THIRD-BASE FALLACY

By far the biggest fallacy I see every day is people getting upset that some-one took a card when they "shouldn't have." And it doesn't matter whether the player is playing first base (the first seat) or third (the last seat). If the person at first base hit his 12 against my 3 (the correct basic-strategy play, by the way), he's ruined the "flow of the cards," created a disturbance in the Force, and may well have ripped the very fabric of space-time itself. People forget that basic strategy was not calculated based on everyone at the table playing as they "should," it was calculated using one top-of-the-deck hand and reshuffling after every play. There is no sacred order of the cards. Take it from me: That person who doesn't "play right" saves the table just as often as he takes the dealer's bust card.

LOOK FOR A GOOD GAME

If you want to win, don't just sidle up to any old blackjack game and start betting. Look for casinos that offer the blackjack rules that'll help you win.

RULES TO LOOK FOR

Every casino offers some type of blackjack, but rules vary from one casino to the next—sometimes even from one table to the next. Most rule changes not only increase the house edge, but they can also make the game a lot less

interesting. You want as many of the following rules as possible at your table but within the table limits your bankroll will allow.

- **Stick with Vegas-style blackjack.** Never play any of the fancy offshoots, such as twenty-first-century blackjack (found in noncasino card rooms), double exposure blackjack, Spanish 21, California blackjack, or any other goofy variation you might find. Trust me, they're bad bets cleverly designed to take more than the usual amount of money.
- **Blackjacks pay 3 to 2.** Never play a game that offers anything else, especially not those sucker 6 to 5 or straight even-money payouts. The casinos are using smoke and mirrors to convince you that anything but 3 to 2 is a good thing—it's not!
- **Dealer stands on soft 17.** Very hard to find but worth it if you do.
- **The fewer decks, the better.** Single decks are better than multiple decks.
- **Double on any two cards.** Some casinos will allow you to double on any two cards, not just 10 or 11.
- **Double after splitting.** If you split your Eights and get a Three, you want to be able to double.
- **Surrender.** You can surrender half your bet when you're in real trouble.
- **Resplitting your Aces.** When you split Aces in most casinos, you're only allowed one card per Ace, no matter what. Look for a casino that lets you split them again if you're dealt another Ace.

PITCH VS. SHOE VS. CSM

Back in the day, blackjack was a single deck game in which the dealer would "pitch" the cards to the player. When counters started winning, the casinos added more decks and had dealers deal the cards face up from a shoe. Nowadays, continuous shuffle machines (CSMs) are in. Here, four to six decks are loaded into a machine that continuously shuffles them as the hands are dealt. These devices make card counters and cheating dealers a thing of the past. But which type of dealing gives you the best chance of winning? Obviously, if the rules are favorable, you should always try to find a single-deck pitch game. The house edge is smaller, mainly because the fewer cards mean you get dealt more blackjacks. If you can't find a true single-deck game (and they're becoming rarer and rarer), it doesn't much matter whether you go with shoes or CSMs. You're looking for that elusive run, and I've seen them in both. I've seen CSMs that get cold and dump the tray to the table, and I've seen customers get clobbered playing shoes, and vice versa. If you follow my other guidelines in this chapter, it really won't matter.

TRENDS

The math nerds say that, in the long run, you can't win at blackjack without counting—all you can hope for, they say, is to lose as little as possible. But you're not looking to lose as little as possible, and you're not looking to play a billion hands of blackjack. You're thinking short term, and you want to win now. And as we talked about in chapter 2, the only way to do that is to catch a hot streak, to experience some of the random variance that separates the losers from the winners. You need to track down the hot tables and cold dealers.

BLACKJACK DEALERS

Casino dealers have good days and bad days, just like everyone else. There are "hot" dealers and "cold" dump trucks (so named because they are dumping the casino's profits out to players). These dealers aren't card mechanics; they're just experiencing good or bad trends. A customer could be doing everything right, but a hot dealer will scoop his money faster than the math nerds say he should.

Dealers are always asking one another during breaks: "How you running?" To which they usually reply: "Man, I'm on fire today, nobody can beat me," or they'll say, "I'm practically dumping my tray today, the cards are so cold." Of course, there are plenty of dealers who are just trending average, going through the usual ups and downs that we all experience from day to day.

MEET "THE PENCIL"

For dealers, the pencil is the most powerful person in the casino. The pencil decides what dealer goes to what table, whether it's the high-limit blackjack or the low-limit roulette tables.

But it's not as simple as merely pulling names out of a hat and sending someone to this or that table. The pencil knows who's skilled and who's a novice, and especially who's running hot and who's cold, not only from day to day but just in general.

When you have a house dealer who always seems to take the players' money, where do you think the pencil will send him? Over to the low-roller table where the highest bet is five bucks, or to the $100 table where Mr. Moneybags is taking the casino for tens of thousands of dollars?

As for the dump trucks, you can rest assured that the pencil is going to put them where they can do the least amount of damage, at the $1 or $5 minimum tables.

FIND A DEALER

The first thing you've got to do is find a table and a dealer. If you've read my advice on bankroll, trends, and the pencil, you'll be paying particular attention to low-limit tables first. Generally speaking, the higher the limit, the better the rules—but the tougher the dealer.

If the dealer's standing by herself, just ask her if she's killing 'em or not. If the dealer's on fire, she'll tell you, in which case you should heed her warning. I've seen scores of players ignore these warnings only to get smoked within minutes.

If, on the other hand, a dealer offers some encouraging words, pull up a chair and give it a whirl. Sure, some people don't like to play one-on-one with the dealer, but the biggest winning streaks I've seen have happened when a customer is playing heads up (one-on-one against the house).

If there are no empty tables, by all means look for a busy one. Just find out whether it's trending good or bad.

- Watch a few hands to see how often the dealer's busting. Is it take-take-take, a bit of back and forth, or are the players winning one hand after another?
- What's the dealer's typical up card? Is it always a face or an Ace? If so, the dealer's probably destroying the table and you'll want to look somewhere else.
- How do the players look? Are they having a good time? Or do they look like they're witnessing their own funerals?
- How many chips do the players have? Is anyone down to his last stack?

If everything indicates you're watching a good table, then sit yourself down and buy in. Just don't get too comfortable.

THREE STRIKES AND YOU'RE OUTTA THERE

In an ideal world, you'd slip a dealer a small tip, and he'd tell you who the hot and cold dealers are. Unfortunately, it doesn't work that way very often. So you've got to keep in mind this rule when playing blackjack:

{ Your Butt Is Not Glued to That Chair }

Every day I hear players constantly complaining about the dealer absolutely killing them, taking all of their money. And then, after losing eight hands in a row, they reach into their wallet and pull out another hundred.

In this case, you've obviously run up against a hot dealer, a hot table, or a hot shoe, any of which is bad for your bankroll. You need to find a cold dealer, cold table, or cold shoe. You need to go on the proverbial run and ride that winning streak, and you ain't gonna do it leaning into the punch that a hot dealer is doling out. So you must adopt this policy if you want to survive:

{ If You Lose 3 Hands in a Row, You Must Change Tables, Period }

Why would you continue to throw good money after bad? Do you think you can will yourself better cards? The only way you're going to get a good run of cards is to find another table, another dealer, another casino, anything! Just get the hell out of there.

Hopefully, you're playing in a large casino with lots of blackjack tables. If you can't find another table, be patient. Take a short walk around the casino. Play a slot machine. Try a different game. Then come back when there's a new dealer, a new shoe, or new people who've been playing. Discipline is the name of the game.

MONEY MANAGEMENT

So you finally find a table that meets all the right criteria, and you decide to sit down to play. You've memorized basic strategy, and you're going to play it religiously. The biggest question now is: How are you supposed to bet?

The math nerds would say that it makes no difference whether you flat bet or change it up; it's all exactly the same in the long run. But years of real-world experience tell me that how you bet is the most important thing! I cannot emphasize enough that the only way to win consistently is by using sound money management.

CATCHING THOSE STREAKS

To win at any table game, you've got to take advantage of that random variation, those trends that we've spent so much time talking about. You're fighting the house edge with every bet, and everything up to this point has prepared you to find the table, dealer, and shoe that'll hopefully let you catch the lucky run that's essential to winning. All your work up to this point has been in preparation for the positive trends. Now that you've found one, you've got to take advantage of it.

THE BLACKJACK BETTING METHOD

1. **Decide on your minimum comfortable bet,** which will be one unit. Whether it's $3, $10, or even $100, simply continue to bet that one unit until you win a hand.
2. **When you win,** increase your next bet by 50 percent. So if your base unit is $10 and you win, your next bet would be $15.
3. **Keep increasing the amount of your winning bets** by that same amount until you've won three hands in a row. Then cap your bets until you lose a hand. For example, a winning progression would look like this: $10, $15, $20, $25, $25, $25, and so on.
4. **Once you lose a hand,** go back to betting your minimum until you win again. Lather, rinse, repeat. Now you're minimizing your losses but taking advantage of the streaks when they do come along.

Of course, not everyone is going to start at $10. Just adjust the progression according to your minimum bet. For example, if you start with a $2 unit, the progression would go: $2, $3, $4, $5, $5.

DOUBLING AND SPLITTING

Here's some advice to keep in mind as you calculate the progression: Regardless of whether you double, split, or push, increase or decrease your bet based on the net win or net loss on each hand.

If you split your pair, then win one but lose the other, you broke even for a push, so you keep the next bet the same. If you lost both splits, you revert back to your base bet. If you split, double, and split some more and you end up ahead, you step up the bet. If you lost money, you revert to the base bet. Obviously, if you get a blackjack, you're ahead, so you increase your bet. If you surrender, it's a loss, so you go back to the beginning.

And don't forget: If you lose three hands in a row, get up and find another table!

BLACKJACK BOOBY TRAPS

Back during the "good ol' days" of Vegas, when the Rat Pack was in full swing and every casino was run by professional hoodlums, you'd be lucky to find a blackjack game, roulette wheel, or craps table that wasn't fixed in some way. And if you nevertheless walked out with a nice chunk of change, the pit boss would often send some of his goons to "escort you to your car."

But ever since Uncle Sam swaggered into Vegas and busted Mafia chops, casinos went corporate, then legitimate, and Vegas's cheating ways became a thing of the past. Nowadays, casinos from here to hoedown have all figured out tricks for taking your money that are entirely legal. Watch out for these common tactics.

CHANGING THE CARDS

The cheap paper cards that casinos use get beat up pretty fast when they're being shuffled 24/7, especially if the customers' grimy mitts have been fondling them for hours, so most casinos change their cards about once a day. Unfortunately, some casinos change them a lot more often.

I remember dealing at a small Indian casino in California when the whole table started winning—a lot. I wasn't doing anything special, just dealing out a strong run of cards. But it didn't take long before my pit boss came over and announced that, even though we'd only opened the game a few hours ago, and that it was the middle of the day, it was time to change the cards . . . all six decks!

So we emptied out all of the fairly new cards, cracked the cases of six fresh decks, shuffled them, and reloaded the CSM. The boss hoped this would change the flow of the cards as well as get impatient players to move to a "winning" table.

Of course, some pit bosses didn't like the hassle of putting in new cards, so they would ask me to "accidentally" hit the power switch on the shuffle machine. This would make it reboot and spit out all the cards, and you'd then have to reload them all over, again changing the flow of the "good" cards.

Another nearby Indian casino had quite the reputation of having dealers "accidentally" drop the deck or the whole shoe, spilling the cards everywhere so they'd have to reload them all over again.

So what do you do if you think something is up? Simple: Change casinos, or at the very least, change tables. Just be on the watch.

CHANGING SHUFFLES

Every casino has what's called a house shuffle, a certain routine that every dealer follows to ensure a consistent, across-the-board shuffle. But if a player or a whole table is winning a lot, some pit bosses discreetly tell the dealer to "change up your shuffle," such as putting in an extra riffle or two, or "scramble them extra good" next time, all in an attempt to get the players to start losing.

CHANGING DEALERS

If a dealer is dumping, pit bosses have been known to pull that dealer off the table and put in one of their hot "house dealers." The dealers aren't cheating; they're just running hot for the day and seem to be taking everyone's money. One time, I was stuck on a table for three times longer than normal because I had the hot hand that day and was allowed to go on break only after I'd "won" enough money back from the customer. Another time, I was yanked after five minutes because it happened to be my lucky day and I was giving away too much money. If you notice that a hot dealer has been there longer than the rest or that they're changing dealers every ten minutes, watch your money and follow the three-strikes rule.

CHAPTER 4

Last time I checked, there were a million different books on poker, all promising to teach you everything you need to know to go from fish to pro in 500 easy pages. And nowadays, thanks to televised poker programs that show Joe Average winning millions of dollars, people are buying up these books by the truck-full and pouring into casinos, desperate to play Texas hold 'em, even if they haven't a clue whether a flush beats a straight.

Sure, I could blather on for the rest of the book detailing the finer points of poker strategy, but instead I'll give you a quick and dirty guide so you can go into a game and win today. Also, I realize that most people reading this book are interested only in one of two types of Texas hold 'em—low-limit poker and no-limit poker—so this chapter will teach you how to win quickly at either.

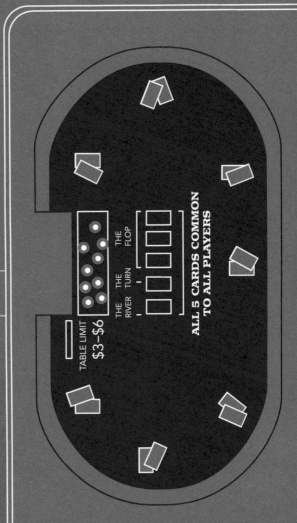

TEXAS HOLD 'EM TABLE

TABLE LIMIT
$3-$6

THE FLOP

THE TURN

THE RIVER

ALL 5 CARDS COMMON
TO ALL PLAYERS

At its heart, poker is about making the best five-card hand, whether you are dealt two cards (Texas hold 'em), four cards (Omaha), or seven cards (seven-card stud). You use five cards and only five, and whoever has the best five cards wins.

So what beats what? Here's the rank of poker hands from lowest to highest:

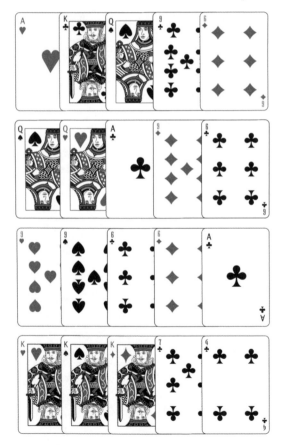

HIGH CARD
If nobody has any of the hands described below, the player with the highest card wins.

ONE PAIR
One pair of the same rank (here shown with an Ace kicker, that is, the highest card after your pair is an Ace).

TWO PAIR
Two pairs of the same rank: Nines and Sixes with an Ace kicker.

THREE OF A KIND
Three cards of the same rank: Kings with a Seven kicker.

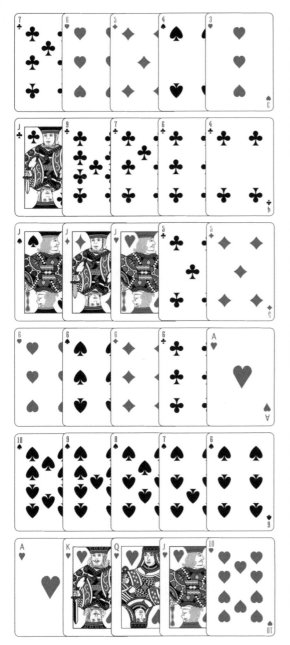

STRAIGHT
Five consecutive cards of varying suits. Since the highest card is a Seven, you'd call this a Seven-high straight.

FLUSH
Five nonconsecutive cards of the same suit.

FULL HOUSE
Includes a three of a kind and a pair in the same hand.

FOUR OF A KIND
Here you have four of a kind with an Ace kicker.

STRAIGHT FLUSH
Five consecutive cards of the same suit. This particular hand is a Ten-high straight flush, an almost unbeatable hand.

ROYAL FLUSH
The unbeatable hand. It occurs only once every 650,000 hands, give or take a few.

A SAMPLE HAND

A typical hold 'em game has you sitting down with up to nine players at a poker table. At the start of the game, one person is designated "the button" —this person gets a circular piece of plastic labeled "dealer" placed in front of him. If you were playing at home, the button would actually deal the cards (thus the dealer label), but at a casino he only gets to enjoy the benefits of being the dealer—that is, he gets to bet last. After each hand is completed and the money, or pot, is pushed to the winner, the button moves clockwise to the next person.

THE BLINDS

In other poker games, everyone has to put an ante, or a small amount of money, into the pot, so that there's some incentive to play a hand. In Texas hold 'em, everyone takes a turn being "the blinds." The person to the immediate left of the button has to post (or bet) what's called the small blind. The person next to the small blind has to post the big blind. These are essentially forced bets that add money to the pot to get things going. How much the blinds have to bet depends on the betting limits or structure of the particular table. For example, the most popular game in card rooms right now is $3–$6 Texas hold 'em. That is, betting and raising are done in increments of $3 for the first two rounds, and $6 for the last two rounds. The big blind is usually the smaller of the two numbers, which in $3–$6 would be $3. The small blind is typically half or less of the big blind—in most $3–$6 games, it's a buck. But don't worry, the casino dealer will tell you exactly how much you need to bet to get the action started.

Except for the two blinds, no one at the table has to post anything.

PRE-FLOP

Once the blinds have been posted, the casino dealer doles out two cards (called hole cards) to each player. Since the blinds have already put in some money, the first person to act is the player to the immediate left of the big blind. He looks at his cards, and if he doesn't like what he sees, he can simply muck his hand, or fold it, by tossing the cards back toward the dealer without having to bet a dime. However, if he wants to stay in the hand with his two cards, he has to bet at least the big blind, which in this case is $3. If he really likes his cards, he can say, "Raise," and up the bet in a single increment of $3. In this case he raises to $6, or as they say, "makes it two bets to go."

The person to the raiser's left looks at his cards, doesn't like them, and mucks his hand. But the next person likes his cards, so he "calls" the raiser's bet and also puts in $6. The next player to act looks at his hand and likes his cards as well, but instead of just calling, he reraises and bets exactly $9, making it "three bets to go." Everyone else folds until betting gets to the button, who calls the $9. Now it's the small blind's turn. He already has $1 in the pot, so he has to bet only $8 more to call the bet, but he figures that's too rich for his blood, so he folds.

Now the action is on the big blind. He only has to put in $6 to call the bet, but he decides to reraise and bets a total of $12, making it four bets to go (his original $3 plus $9 more). At this point, the betting would usually be capped, that is, nobody else could raise the betting to $15, as the maximum number of raises per round is typically three or four, depending on which casino you're visiting. All the other players decide to call the $12 and fork over the extra chips.

THE FLOP

After making sure that everyone has bet correctly, the dealer scoops all the money into the middle and then places three cards face up in the center of the table. These cards are collectively called the flop and are community cards that any of the remaining players can use with their two cards to make the best five-card hand. Of course, they keep in mind that there are still two more community cards to come.

After the flop, the first person to act is the player to the left of the button. The three cards "on the board," or the center of the table, don't help his

hand much, so since he's first to act, he decides not to bet and simply taps his hand on the table and says, "Check," which means the action goes to the next person. The second player doesn't care for the flop either and says, "Check," as well. However, the next guy does like it and decides to bet the minimum $3. The button raises to $6, and everyone else calls.

Now the dealer turns over one more card, called the turn (though in some antiquated circles it's called Fourth Street). Now the betting has doubled and starts at $6 (remember, we're sitting at a $3–$6 table). The first player bets $6, and the next player raises it to $12 (raising in the last two rounds needs to be done in increments of $6). Instead of calling or raising, the remaining players fold, except for the first bettor, who calls $12. Now that there are only two players left going into the final round, they're considered to be playing heads up.

The dealer turns over the fifth and final card, the river (or as some say, Fifth Street), and signals to the first player to make a decision. He bets $6, and the only other player raises to $12. The first player reraises to $18, to which the second player responds by reraising to $24. In most card rooms, the action would be capped after three raises, but when the round's heads up, unlimited raising and reraising is typically allowed. The first player simply calls, and with that, both players turn over their cards, and everyone sees who has the best five-card hand using the players' hole cards plus the community cards. Who-ever has the best cards gets pushed the entire pot. In the rare event of a tie, the pot is "chopped," or evenly split, and each player gets an equal share.

LIMIT VS. NO-LIMIT

What we've been talking about is your basic structured-limit Texas hold 'em. The amount you're allowed to bet and raise is all predetermined. You can find $2–$4 limit games, $250–$500 limit games, and everything in between—but in every case, the amount you can bet is still predetermined.

However, the poker most people see on television is called no-limit Texas hold 'em, in which, as the name implies, you can essentially bet whatever you have in front of you at any time, whether it's $50 or $10,000.

Of course, it'd be fairly obscene to pit a player of limited means against a millionaire who could bully him around with stacks of $1,000 chips, so almost all no-limit games have minimum and maximum buy-ins. For example, a small no-limit game might have a $50–$200 buy-in, meaning that you must bring at least $50 in chips to the table, but you can't start with more than $200.

But just because the minimum buy-in is $50 or $100 doesn't mean that the blinds are that high. They're usually something reasonable, like $5 or $10.

HOW BETTING WORKS IN NO-LIMIT

After the blinds have been posted, the first person to act has three choices: She can fold, call the big blind, or raise, which must be at least double the big blind. So if the big blind is $5, when the first player raises, she must make her bet at least $10. Of course, most people who raise in no-limit like to bet at least three to five times the big blind—that's why they're playing no-limit. The first player could announce that she wants to go all-in, but she probably wouldn't get many callers that way and would end up winning only the few bucks from the blinds.

After someone has raised, the next person also has the same three options: he can fold, he can call the $15, or he can raise by at least doubling whatever the most recent bet was. Again, at any time, and usually after there's been a fair amount of action, you can go all-in, which means that whoever wants to call you has to bet at least as much as you put in. Of course, if he doesn't have enough to cover your action, or not enough to raise by doubling your bet, he simply goes all-in with whatever he has. So if someone goes all in with $100 against another player's $1,000, the short stack can win only as much as he bet from each player who called him—in this case, $100.

PLAN OF ATTACK

Tons of books have been written about chess strategy. Hell, whole libraries have been written just on the game's opening moves. Like chess, poker has numerous nuances that a single chapter can't cover and plenty of intricacies that can be learned only from experience.

But I can show you what you need to know to get started (and win) today, whether you choose low-limit hold 'em or no-limit hold 'em.

NO FOLD 'EM HOLD 'EM

Low-limit hold 'em is often called no fold 'em hold 'em because most players will keep their lousy hands until all of the cards are drawn, hoping that the river (or fifth card) will deliver a miracle. You want these people sitting at your table, because they're the ones who are going to feed your games. They're the ones who will make playing poker profitable for you. Sure, there will be days when they get lucky and take all of your buy-ins. But if you stick with your game plan, you'll be ready to pounce once their luck runs out.

Poker is a game of patience, especially if you're playing limit hold 'em. You have to be willing to sit and wait for the good cards to come. Most people don't have the patience, and after mucking hand after hand they decide to start playing anything that looks even semidecent, with predictable results. You need to wait until you're dealt strong starting cards before you can even think about entering the hand.

So what makes a good starting hand? It's actually fairly simple. I tell every beginner and even some experienced players to stick with these guidelines, period.

STARTING HAND REQUIREMENTS

Poker is about percentages. You need to play hands that have a higher than normal percentage of winning. If you play only hands that have high winning percentages against foolish players who play anything, you're naturally going to win more often than not. It's as easy as that.

Out of the 169 different starting hands you can be dealt, don't even consider putting your money out there unless you are dealt:

- **Any pocket pair.** Both of your cards are the same rank—pocket Twos all the way up to pocket Aces
- **Ace-King.** Either both of the same suit (suited) or different suits (unsuited)
- **Ace-Queen.** Either suited or unsuited
- **King-Queen.** Either suited or unsuited

If you get any other hand, throw it away.

ARE YOU SERIOUS?

Now I'm sure every aspiring poker player is screaming that if they were to follow the above advice they'll practically be throwing in every hand. And my response is: Absolutely! If you're playing more than 1 out of every 4 hands, you're playing way too many.

Of course, we've all seen people who play a lot of hands, and sometimes they get lucky. Some people's hold-'em strategy is "any two will do," meaning that no one knows how good their hand really is until after the flop. But that's financial suicide. Sure, those people will win with garbage once in a while. But these same people always, always, always give their money back eventually. You just have to be patient and wait for their luck to turn.

Now, you all know I'm not a big fan of math nerds and their relentless calculations, but in this case my experience shows that they know what they're talking about. Having run billions of computer simulations, they've proven which starting hands consistently win against other starting hands. This is reality, and you ignore it at your own peril.

TIGHT MAKES RIGHT

Generally speaking, the fewer hands you play, the more you'll win. But do I expect you to take these starting hand requirements to the World Series of Poker? Of course not. These starting hands are for beginners (or losers who think they know what they're doing but just keep losing), before you discover the subtleties of the game. There's only so much you can read from books, and without real-world experience, you'll never get any better. Stick with these starting hands until you've got at least 200 hours under your belt. And even then, you should consider playing more hands only on very rare occasions.

IF THE POT'S BEEN RAISED PRE-FLOP

Just because those are the starting-hand requirements doesn't mean that they'll work in every situation. If a player has already raised before you even get a chance to bet, you need to seriously consider folding your hand.

If someone before you has raised, it usually means that he's got something good, so he's more likely to win. You should call his raise only if you have something equally intimidating, which to be honest, ain't pocket deuces. If the pot has not only been raised but reraised, you've got at least two people with very strong starting hands, and you should only call with premium cards (more on this in a moment). Calling with a weak hand is just plain stupid. Sure, you could catch that miracle flop, but nine times out of ten, you'll just be donating money to someone else's bankroll.

Some people like to play certain goofy combinations that they seem to "always win with," like Ten-Six suited or everyone's favorite, Six-Nine. And true, any two cards can get lucky once in awhile, but if you keep playing those rags, you're going to go broke sooner rather than later.

The next two pages offer a general recap of when to call, bet, raise, reraise. If you don't meet any of the criteria shown here, you must fold.

IF THE POT HASN'T BEEN RAISED, bet or call with these hands or higher:

IF THE POT HAS BEEN RAISED ONCE, call with these hands:

IF THE POT HAS BEEN RERAISED, call with these hands:

IF THE POT HAS BEEN CAPPED, call with these hands:

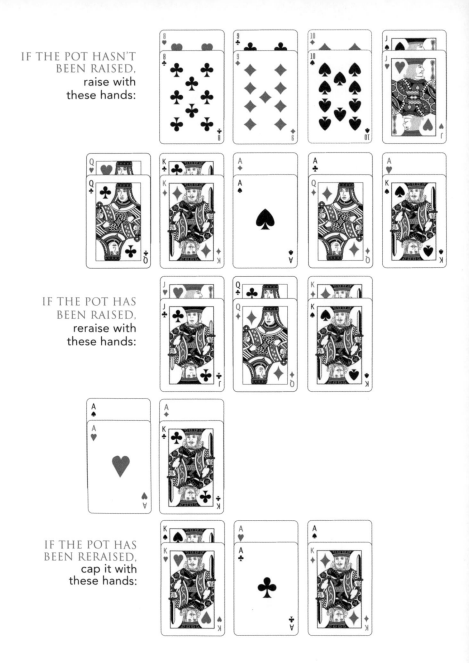

IF THE POT HASN'T
BEEN RAISED,
**raise with
these hands:**

IF THE POT HAS
BEEN RAISED,
**reraise with
these hands:**

IF THE POT HAS
BEEN RERAISED,
**cap it with
these hands:**

BLUFFING

Obviously, if people are staying to the river with horrible hands, it almost makes no sense to try to bluff somebody out of a pot with a bad hand. In all likelihood, they're going to call you. Unless you know someone is extremely tight, there's really no sense in trying to bluff, as it only costs a couple of bucks to "play Sheriff" and see if you actually do have what you're representing. Bluffing really doesn't become part of poker unless you're playing in higher limits or playing no-limit.

AFTER THE FLOP

Every poker guru in the world has his own strategy for what to do after the flop, but you just need to consider the following simple questions.

Did Anyone Raise Before the Flop?

If they did, they probably did so with a good hand, like Ace-something or a pocket pair. You've got to watch how these people react to the flop and try to determine if they got their desired hand.

Are There Over Cards?

Are there any cards on the flop higher than the cards you have? If so, you've got to figure that somebody else probably paired up, especially if he bets into you. If that's the case, you've got to seriously consider folding.

Is This a Worst-Case Scenario?

If the flop has three cards to a flush or straight, you've got to figure at least one of your opponents is probably on a draw (that is, they're hoping to get another card that'll make their hand). You've always got to think to yourself: What does that guy have that will beat me? Is he betting like he's got a three of a kind? If the board is paired, does he act like he's got a full house?

Are You in Love with a Bad Hand?

You may have started out with a superior hand, but after the flop, everything could have changed. If you had pocket Jacks and another person stayed in with Ace-Five off suit, you were looking pretty good before the flop. But when the flop comes Six-Six-Ace, your Jacks have become almost worthless. Not only are the odds fairly good that someone has another Ace, but someone else may very well have a Six. Even though you've gone hours without seeing a decent hand, you've got to be willing to throw those Jacks away if anyone is showing any strength in their betting. Never fall in love with a hand. If you've got a pair of Aces and there's four to a straight and a flush on the board, and everybody is still betting, to call or raise would just be throwing money away. Don't be afraid to fold your hand. Your bankroll will thank you later.

AFTER YOUR FIRST 200 HOURS

Once you've become a consistent, winning player (and by *consistent* I mean you win at least three out of every five sessions), you can start adding a few more hands to your play list. But keep in mind that the more hands you add, the bigger the swings you'll have. When you win, you'll generally win more. And when you lose, you'll lose more often and lose more money. But hey, you've got to grow up sometime. If the pot hasn't been raised, I hereby give you permission to limp in with:

- **Ace plus anything suited,** such as Ace-Three suited
- **Suited face cards,** like Jack-King of Spades
- **Suited connectors** (two cards of consecutive rank and the same suit) Six-Seven or higher

NO-LIMIT HOLD 'EM

Players who grow tired of no fold 'em hold 'em often get frustrated and think that no-limit is the best way to play. They think that in $3–$6 you can't push someone off a pot because it's only costing your opponents a few bucks to try to catch the one card in the deck that can save them. In no-limit, they can bet $100 with a good hand and drive those river rats out.

Although that's true to a point, no-limit is not "real" poker. No-limit is lazy poker. It's for people who don't have the patience to wait for the good starting hands to come along and want to bully people around at the table with their chips. And if that's the way they approach no-limit, they're going to quickly find themselves broke by the more experienced players.

But there is a way to quickly jump into the world of no-limit poker without worrying about things like pot odds and other minutiae. Just follow this simple no-limit betting method to start winning immediately:

1. **Buy in for as little as you can.** Whatever the minimum buy-in is, go with that. If it's a $50–$200 no-limit table, buy only $50. You want to appear as nonthreatening as possible.

2. **Play only the absolute best hands.** Don't even consider anything less than pocket Eight-Eight—and if anyone has raised pre-flop, it'll take an amazing hand to keep you from folding.

3. **If you're the first to act,** raise five times the big blind.

4. **After the flop,** you're either going to fold or go all-in.

That's it. You're only going to make two bets: one before the flop and one after. And with this method, not only is it profitable, it's also extremely tough to defend against.

IF YOU'RE FIRST TO ACT, raise with:

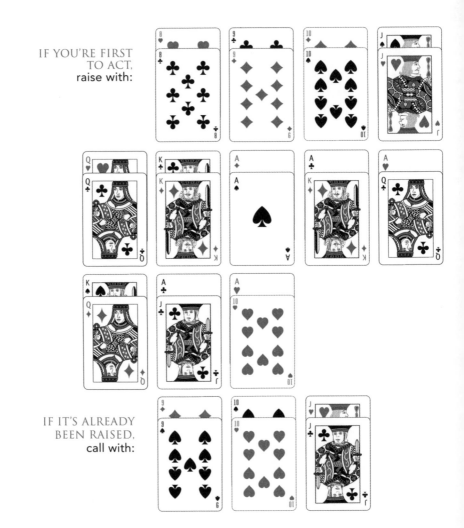

IF IT'S ALREADY BEEN RAISED, call with:

IF IT'S ALREADY
BEEN RAISED,
reraise with:

IF IT'S ALREADY
BEEN RE-RAISED,
call with:

WATCH THE FLOP

If the flop comes and it completely misses you, giving nothing but overcards (cards higher than yours), or if it possibly makes a flush or obvious straight, then you should consider folding. But if there's nothing threatening on the board, then push it all-in. Since you are short stacked, the others in the pot will feel you're pretty safe and worth the call, even if they might not have the best hand. But since you play only when you do have the best hand, this is an extremely profitable method of doubling your stack. Once you've doubled or tripled your stack, consider leaving. You're no longer the short stack at the table and players will be intimidated. Go home and enjoy your winnings.

MONEY MANAGEMENT

If you've followed my bankroll advice, you came to the poker game with 100 times your smallest bet, so for a $3–$6 you came with $300. I've seen people come to a $3–$6 game and buy in for the minimum of $30. Now, what do they expect to do with that kind of money? Are they going to raise or reraise when they should? If they finally get pocket aces, are they going to have the stacks to be able to build the pot? Of course not. You need to have enough money to get started and a little bit to reload if you suffer a bad beat or two. Playing against other players rather than the casino is no excuse to play until you're completely out of money. If things go south, you still need to walk away with a little bit of something besides your pride. So I recommend that once you're down to only 20 times your smallest bet, pick up your chips and cash out with money still left in your pocket. You may have taken a beating, but by God, they didn't take you for everything.

If you're winning, on the other hand, I recommend not leaving—until you start losing. Your minimum goal is to double your buy-in and, ideally, to triple it. Hopefully you aren't being stupid and betting with bad cards simply to play your rush. Don't throw your chips away. Once you've doubled your money (or better), be prepared to leave if you give back half of the winnings. Again, you might say to yourself, "But maybe I'll catch another run of cards." But maybe you'll just end up giving back all of it, and then you'll be kicking yourself for not leaving with some profits.

CHAPTER 5

Rumor has it that the French mathematician who invented roulette either (a) went insane trying to figure out a way to beat it, (b) eventually committed suicide after failing to beat it, or (c) some combination of the two. Since then, millions of gamblers have killed countless brain cells trying to come up with a sure-fire system to beat the wheel. I mean, how hard could it be? It's just a simple wheel with 37 numbers on it, right? But this elegant game has lured many a man into bankruptcy.

ROULETTE WHEEL AND TABLE

The American roulette wheel sports 38 numbered pockets, alternating between black and red (except for the green 0 and 00), though not in chronological order. The croupier (a fancy word for "roulette dealer") spins a tiny ball (sometimes called a pill) one way while the wheel turns the other way. Wherever the ball lands is the winning number. Easy, peasy.

Next to the roulette wheel is a layout featuring all the numbers on the wheel, including the green 0 and 00. If you bet a single number, you're betting that number straight up, and if it wins, you'll be paid 35 to 1. This would be pretty dull if that was all there was to it, so you're allowed to bet any number of other, less lucrative bets. You can bet whether the winning number will be black or red, odd or even, or high or low. You can bet on two, three, four, or six numbers at once, or if a number will appear in a particular column. Following is a list of bets along with their corresponding payouts:

 INSIDE BETS

(A) Straight Up: Bet on a single number, with the chip bet completely on one square and no other. You can even bet on the green 0 or 00. Pays 35 to 1.

(B) Split: A bet on two adjoining numbers, either on the vertical or horizontal (as in 11-14 or 8-9). Pays 17 to 1.

(C) Street: A bet placed on three numbers on a single horizontal row. Pays 11 to 1.

(D) Corner (or square): A bet on four numbers in a square layout (as in 22-23-25-26). The chip is placed at the horizontal and vertical intersection of these numbers. Pays 8 to 1.

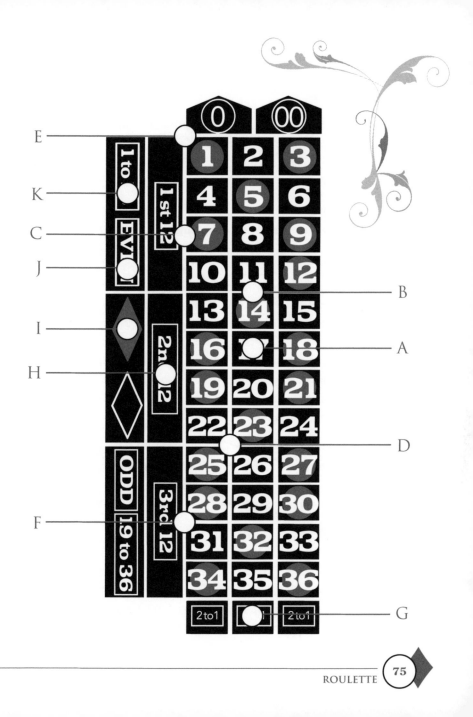

(E) The Five-Number Bet: The worst bet on the roulette table. Includes a bet on 0, 00, 1, 2, and 3. Pays 6 to 1 and has a house edge 50 percent higher than any other bet.

(F) Double Street (Six-Number Bet, Line Bet): A bet on two adjoining streets, with the chip placed at the corresponding intersection (as in 25-30). Pays 5 to 1.

 OUTSIDE BETS

On the outer fringes of the layout are the outside bets, which pick whole sets of numbers, though you won't win any of these bets if 0 or 00 hit.

(G) Columns: This is a bet on all 12 numbers on any of the three vertical lines (such as 1-4-7-10 on down to 34). The chip is placed on the space below the final number in this string and includes neither 0 nor 00. Pays 2 to 1.

(H) Dozens: A bet placed on the first dozen numbers (1–12), the second dozen (13–24), or the third dozen (25–36). These also don't include either the 0 or 00. Pays 2 to 1.

 EVEN MONEY BETS

The lowest-paying bets offer a roughly 50-50 shot at winning (actually it's 47.3 percent by factoring in the green zeroes). You can bet red or black (I), odd or even (J), or high (19–36) or low (1–18) numbers (K). Each one pays even money, or 1 to 1.

 HOUSE EDGE

I know what you're thinking: Surely there must be some bet that's better than the others. But alas, there is not. As I discussed in a bit more detail in the house edge section of chapter 1, there are 38 numbers altogether, but we're only getting paid 35 to 1, so every single bet (except for the 5-line bet) has a steep house edge of 5.26. And that 5-line bet (covering 1, 2, 3, 0, and 00) has a house edge of 7.89 percent!

 GREEDY CAPITALIST PIGS

Right now you might be asking, "Why is roulette so popular around the world when the house edge is so terrible?" For starters, you need to understand that I'm talking about the house edge for roulette in the United States—it's nearly triple the house edge in casinos throughout Europe.

You see, the European roulette wheel has only a single 0, giving it 37 numbers instead of our 38 and a house edge of only 2.70 percent.

But wait, there's more:

THE "EN PRISON" RULE

On many a European wheel, the "en prison" rule is common, though it only counts for even-money bets. When the winning number is the green 0, some casinos will allow the player to reclaim half the original bet or to leave the bet (*en prison* = "in prison") for another roulette spin, hoping that the next spin will be a winner. If you leave it and the wheel comes up 0 again, you lose the whole bet.

PLAN OF ATTACK

It's said that there is a roulette system for every European—everybody brags that they've got a can't-miss system for beating the wheel (especially if they're trying to sell you said system).

There are essentially two types of systems that people try to use in beating the wheel: mathematical and physical.

MATHEMATICAL SYSTEMS

Within days of playing roulette, everyone seems to develop some sort of mathematical system to win, something they think millions of others have overlooked but their unheralded genius has managed to devise within moments.

A mathematical system is a method of betting nearly each and every spin but using some sort of negative progression to recoup your current losses. The simplest is the Martingale. You pick a color, such as red, and you merely double your bet each time you lose. Eventually, so the reasoning goes, you'll win and get all your money back plus your original wager, right? Well, actually, no! For a detailed discussion on why the Martingale is a horrible system, jump ahead to chapter 13. Otherwise, just know that every casino has a table limit that you can't bet past. So if you lose more than eight times in a row, the table limits will keep you from doubling your bet again.

Then there's the Labouchere, the d'Alembert, the Fibonacci, the Paroli, and quite literally a million others. If you want to know how many roulette systems there are, simply type "roulette system" into Google, and you'll see every possible progression imaginable, all for the low, low price of a few thousand dollars.

Trying to use math to beat the math (which in this case is the house edge) is like trying to fight fire with kerosene. You can't win.

PHYSICAL SYSTEMS

Physical systems try to exploit weaknesses not in the math but in the mechanics of the wheel itself.

ROULETTE WHEEL BIAS

Rumor has it, especially with older wheels, that the rotors deteriorate, pockets become worn, and frets get loosened. When this happens, the formerly random roulette wheel will become "biased" and start to favor certain sections or even certain numbers. Instead of coming up once every 38 spins, a spongy slot or the worn frets around it will cause a number to win once every 30 spins or so. At least in theory.

Hallelujah! You've found El Dorado! Now all you have to do is get out your pad and paper and record, oh, about 3,000 or so spins of a particular wheel (that's the minimum it'd take to find a bias). At roughly one spin for every two minutes, it should take you only about 100 hours of continuous observation before you'd want to draw any conclusions. Of course, God forbid after 100 hours you realize that this particular wheel doesn't have an exploitable bias, so you have to find another wheel and start all over again.

And if you did manage to find a biased wheel, hope that the ever-vigilant casino personnel didn't replace it, rotate it, or even schedule its usual weekly maintenance, any of which would throw all of your observations out the window. Was roulette bias ever a profitable strategy? Absolutely. But with today's precision-machined wheels and constant maintenance standards, finding a biased wheel is about as easy as finding a Mensa membership card at a *Larry the Cable Guy* show.

DEALER SIGNATURE

The mindless drudgery of a roulette dealer's life is the key to this particular strategy. After dealing for eight hours a day, five days a week, and however many years in a row, certain roulette dealers will cruise on autopilot, spinning the ball exactly the same way every single time. The informed player need simply spot one of these dealers, study his methods, and then predict roughly where the ball is going to land.

Sounds good in theory. But if you've spent much time playing roulette, you see that dealers don't just spend hours upon hours spinning the roulette wheel. The dealer is talking with customers or being talked to by pit bosses. He's gathering chips, taking care of customers' buy-ins, flirting with the cocktail waitress, or doing any number of other things. Not to mention that he's probably watching how you play.

I worked with one dealer who'd dealt for years in Europe and a few of the high-limit rooms in Vegas. He said that every time he thought people were trying to find a pattern or watch his spins, he'd intentionally change things up a bit, like spin the wheel faster or shoot the ball a little slower.

In a similar vein, there's the strongly held belief that a few expert roulette dealers can control where the ball lands. While I'm not saying that this is absolutely impossible, I do keep in mind the following: In order for the dealer to control the outcome, he must get the roulette wheel spinning at just the right speed, then shoot the ball in the complete opposite direction, have it avoid all the frets and other objects that are on the roulette wheel and have the ball bounce just right to land within a spot or two of the number. That's like Michael Jordan making freethrows while the basketball net is moving in one direction and the floor he's standing on is moving in the other direction. Again, I'm not saying it's completely impossible, but it's not something you want to plan your fortunes around.

WHEEL TRACKING

Finally, there's wheel tracking, which is simply watching the ball and the wheel and calculating approximately at what quarter or section of the wheel the ball is likely to land. Now there are many a story of teams coming in with hidden computers and taking the casino for a bit of money—but here in the good old U. S. of A., using a computer in a casino will get you thrown into prison for cheating.

However, if you like the challenge and don't get dizzy easily, there are players who devote themselves to visually tracking the wheel. Some seem to have almost an innate sense of where a ball will go simply by watching the speed of the wheel and the speed of the ball and then quickly placing their bets appropriately. For those who can do it, more power to you. But I get sick riding in the backseat of a car, so I've never been able to master this method.

HOW CASINOS GET YOU TO LOSE AT ROULETTE

Pit bosses keep a few extra strategies in reserve just to throw you off your game if they think you're winning too much. First we'll tell the dealer to speed things up. Instead of leisurely chatting with the guests and giving everyone plenty of time to make their favorite bets and then some, we'll tell him to speed up his game. This only makes sense for the casino because the more decisions are made per hour, the more that house edge works, and the more money the house makes. Now the dealer will be calling "no more bets" a lot sooner, and you won't be able to take your time to make those bets, throwing off your pace and messing with your game.

Another trick is to merely tell the dealer to change the pill (ball), which most casinos carry in three different sizes. Naturally, it'll bounce and land a bit differently depending on which ball is being used, and your former method of prediction will have to be revised.

SO WHAT'S THE BEST SYSTEM?

There are two things you must keep in mind if you want any shot of winning at roulette.

First, you need to find a trend. One look at a roulette scoreboard will show you how streaky the game is. You can see at a glance whether the table has been favoring red or black, high or low, and so on. You can even see if it's "choppy," that is, if it's doing a lot of back and forth, with the only trend being no trend. The only way you're going to win at roulette is to find a trend and quickly exploit it.

Second, you need to get in and get out fast. The weakness in almost every system is that you stay at the table spin after spin, letting the house edge eventually catch up to you and suck away all your money. The longer you stay at any game, the more likely you are to lose, so you need to hit and run. Find the trend, exploit it, and then get out when things go bad.

These three systems will help you do exactly that.

SYSTEM 1: FOLLOW THE TREND

After finding a table that seems to be streaking, you're going to buy in and bet on one of the even-money wagers (red-black, high-low, even-odd), whichever one seems to be streaking. You look at the last three decisions and bet the one that has won twice. So if the last three decisions are red-black-red, you'd bet two units on red. If it wins, you're going to lock up a profit and drop your bet down to one unit on red, as it's still the color that's won the last two out of three decisions. If it wins again, you're going to bump your betting back up to two units, following the positive progression of 2, 1, 2, 3, 4, 5. If it loses, you simply place a two unit bet on black now, as it's the color that has won the last two out of three decisions.

Key point: Don't ever bounce back and forth between red-black to high-low to odd-even. Pick an even-money bet and stick with it while at this particular table. You'll drive yourself bananas if you keep going back and forth.

SYSTEM 2: CATCH A STREAK

This one is fun if you want to capitalize on streaks before they hit. Pick an even-money bet and bet both sides. I know that by betting on both you can't make a profit on any single decision, but we're looking for streaks here, remember? After every decision, one of your bets will have won and one will have lost. Replace the losing wager and let the winning bet ride with the winnings. On any streak that develops, you'll be there from the absolute beginning. Streaks of three are very common and occur about once every seven decisions. So after a third win, take your profits off and start over.

SYSTEM 3: BET THE DOZENS

This method is great if you really want a slow-paced experience. It's perfect if you want to enjoy a few free drinks and soak in the casino experience. You merely place one unit on the first dozen and one unit on the second dozen, then spin. You've covered 66 percent of the board, so you technically have only a 33 percent chance of losing. Best-case scenario: One of the dozens you picked will hit, paying you 2 to 1. You lose the other bet, so now you're up one unit. Worst-case scenario: Neither dozen hits, and you're down two units.

Streaking dozens are a lot rarer than the even-money bets, but you still

---

want to get in on a trend. So put your primary one-unit bet on whichever dozen won last. For your second bet, try to bet the first dozen (the numbers are more equally spread out around the wheel) or the dozen that hit the last time. So, for example, say 22 just hit. I would put my primary one-unit bet on the second dozen and put one unit on the first dozen. If the next spin loses by hitting, say, 32, my next bet would be one unit on the third dozen and one unit on the first dozen.

If my bet wins, however, I simply collect my winnings and continue playing the same one-unit bets. I never raise or lower my bet with this system.

MONEY MANAGEMENT

The idea is simple: You need to walk away if you've lost five decisions in a row or have lost ten units altogether. Simply find another table or another game. If you find yourself winning, and hopefully have won twenty units, you should be prepared to leave. Of course, you don't want to leave while you're still winning, but if you end up losing half your profits, it's time to take a break. Enjoy your winnings. Buy something nice with it, even if it's only enough to pay for lunch. At least you can say you've walked away a roulette winner, which is more than 99 percent of players can say.

CHAPTER 6

Craps is easily the most exciting and most intimidating game in any casino. People are yelling and throwing money all over the layout, which looks like some sort of crazy puzzle. There are dozens of different bets, all with weird payouts and governed by complicated rules. At least, that's probably the way a newbie sees it.

But at its most basic level, craps is a very simple game. Think of it like this: Every year when the Super Bowl is played, there is really one big, easy bet, and that's on who is going to win the game. But if you're a gambler, you know that Vegas books all kinds of kooky bets (called prop bets), such as betting which team scores the first touchdown, which player rushes for the most yards, who receives the opening kickoff, and so on. Nearly all these bets are long shots and are pretty bad.

It's the same with craps. You can make the simple, boring, and profitable bet, or you can go nuts and bet on just about anything, like whether the next 8 will be rolled 4-4 or 5-3. Trust me: You want to stick with only two or three bets, tops. They may not be as "exciting" as some of the others, but unless you consider going bankrupt "exciting," you'll be much better off sticking with the basics.

Craps

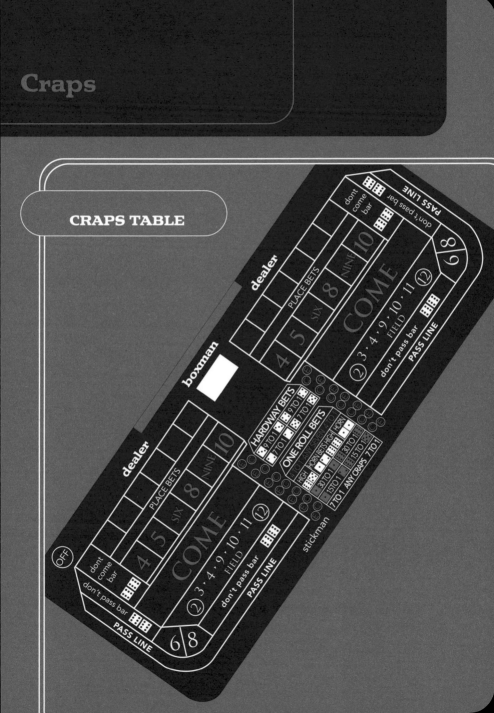

In a nutshell, craps is merely about rolling a certain number. The shooter, the person throwing the dice, is trying to either repeat a previously rolled number, called the point, or roll a seven, depending on how he bets. That's it. Of course, the casino will let you make all kinds of other crazy bets in the meantime, but we'll get to those in a minute.

 ## THE DICE

The dice are key to craps, so you need to know a bit about them to distinguish the bad bets from the not-as-bad bets.

Craps is played with two standard, six-sided dice similar to the ones that come in a children's board game, except they're machine-manufactured to perfection. When a shooter throws the dice, the important number is the sum of the amounts face up on each die. For example, if the shooter rolls a 4 on one die and a 3 on the other, the number is 7, and the bets are paid or removed based on that number.

There are only 11 possible numbers (2 through 12) and only 36 ways of making them.

SEVEN IS KEY

Notice that there are more ways to roll a 7 than any other number (followed very closely by 6 and 8). Craps is built around the number 7, for better and worse. For every 36 rolls, 7 should show up an average of 6 times. The true odds listed above will show you the probability of hitting any number; out of 36 rolls, for example, the number 12 should show up only once.

Notice also that the true odds are for all the different combinations. This is what a bet *should* pay—and when you compare what it *should* pay to what it

#	WAYS TO ROLL	POSSIBLE COMBINATIONS	TRUE ODDS
2	1		35 to 1
3	2		17 to 1
4	3		11 to 1
5	4		8 to 1
6	5		6.2 to 1
7	6		5 to 1
8	5		6.2 to 1
9	4		8 to 1
10	3		11 to 1
11	2		17 to 1
12	1		35 to 1

does pay, you'll start to understand why many of the casino's offerings are bad bets.

Now that you know a bit about the dice, let's play a round.

A TYPICAL GAME

A typical craps layout can have up to 12 people comfortably gathered around it, though if it's a hot table, you can squeeze in more. All players get a chance to roll the dice as long as they've got money on the main bets, the pass line, or the don't pass, but you'll win or lose whether you're rolling or not. Whoever's rolling will keep rolling until they lose. If you don't want to roll the dice when it's your turn, just signal the stickman and he'll push the dice to the next player.

A new round starts when there's a new shooter, and the puck in the corner of the table is turned over to "off." Before the first roll of the dice, or the come-out roll, players are invited to place their bets. We place $10 on the pass line, which is the main bet and best bet (with a low house edge of only 1.41 percent) and within easy reach of every player. The stickman pushes us several dice to choose from, and we pick two to roll with. Using only one hand, we throw the dice to the opposite end of the table, making sure that they bounce off the back wall to keep the roll random.

On the come-out roll, everyone who bet the pass line is hoping that you roll a 7 or an 11, also called a natural, as they're automatic winners. The only numbers you don't want to roll are 2, 3, and 12—these are called craps and are all automatic losers. But let's imagine that you happily oblige the crowd by rolling a 7. The dealer will pay you $10, and then it's time to roll again. On your next roll, you get an 8, so the dealer turns the puck over to "on" and places it above the 8. Nobody who bet the pass line loses or wins anything on this turn, but the point has been established as 8.

To win now, you simply need to repeat the number and roll an 8 again. In fact, you can roll any other number, even the formerly forbidden 2, 3, and 12, but you cannot roll a 7. On the come-out roll, nearly everyone roots for you to roll a 7, but after the point is established, the rolls reverse, and nearly everyone, especially the pass-line bettors, will lose if you roll a 7. In fact, after the point is established, it's considered extremely bad luck for any player to even say the word *seven* during the roll.

And on it goes: You can roll lots of numbers—4, 6, 2, 12, and 6—without winning or losing anything. Since your bet is on the pass line, the only numbers you need to worry about are 7 and 8 (the point). Thankfully, you roll an 8, so everyone who bet the pass line (including you) gets paid, the puck gets turned to "off," and a new come-out roll starts.

You leave your original $10 on the pass line and roll again. This time you roll a 3 craps, and automatically lose your pass-line bet but get to hold the dice for another round. You place $10 on the pass line again and roll several 7s in a row, automatically winning your pass line bet each time. Finally, you roll a 6, making that the point. Your next three rolls are 4, 8, and 9 before you finally roll the dreaded 7. When the 7 hits, all pass line bets lose (and many other bets that we'll get to later), the dice pass to the next shooter, and everyone gets ready for another come-out roll.

And that's it! If you never learned anything else about craps and only bet the pass line just as I described, you'd be better off than nine out of ten craps players, and you'd probably make more than 99 out of 100 craps players ever have. And if everyone bet just the pass line, there's no way the casinos would be able to stay in business.

BUT SURELY THERE'S MORE

Yes, unfortunately. There is much more to the game of craps for those brave souls who are willing to do a bit of digging. But let me say right up front that 90 percent of everything else about craps is crap. We can delve a little deeper into how to wring a bit more value out of your pass line bet, and there are a few other reasonably lucrative bets on the table—but trust me, the rest of the game is garbage.

Remember back in chapter 1 where I explained how the casino makes its money thanks to the house edge? Simply put, it's by paying you less than what the odds of the bet say they should pay. So if the odds are 5 to 1 of something happening, the casino will pay you only 4 to 1. But there is one, and only one, bet in the entire casino that, believe it or not, will pay you true odds, exactly as you should get paid; the casino makes no money on the wager whatsoever, and it's the only bet where the odds aren't against you. And that's the free-odds bet in craps.

Not surprisingly, you won't see the free-odds bet written anywhere on the layout, and you won't usually hear the casino staff encouraging you to take it, but smart gamblers know it's there and know how to play it.

FREE ODDS ON THE PASS LINE

After the point has been established, the player has the option to essentially increase her pass-line bet by "taking odds," that is, by laying another bet directly behind her original pass-line bet. How much she can bet varies from casino to casino, but most offer at least double odds, which means you can bet two times what your pass-line bet is as odds. So if you bet $5 on the pass line, you can put an additional $10 behind it so that you have $15 in action. But wait, there's more. With a simple pass line bet, you get paid even money —$5 won for $5 bet. But with odds, you get paid what you're actually supposed to be paid based on the likelihood of the point number being rolled:

The Point	Payout	Example
4 and 10	2 to 1	a $5 wager is paid $10
5 and 9	3 to 2	a $6 wager is paid $9
6 and 8	6 to 5	a $5 wager is paid $6

So if you have $5 on the pass line when the point is a 6 and you take double odds ($10), when the shooter makes his point (repeats a 6 roll), you'll get paid $5 on the pass-line bet but $12 on the odds bet.

Even better, the more odds you bet, the lower the house edge. You see, your basic pass-line bet has a house edge of 1.41 percent, but the free odds has no house edge. So combining the two lowers the house edge of your original bet. This is one case where the bigger your bet, the lower the odds against you.

Most smart gamblers will figure out what they want their minimum bet to be for a craps session and put as much of it on free odds as possible. So if you figure you don't want to place more than $15 a bet, put $5 on the pass line and place double odds of $10 behind that bet. If everyone made nothing but this bet all day, in short order there would be no more casinos. Not because it's a moneymaker for the players (it still has a house edge, even if it's extremely small), it's just that the casinos make hardly enough money off it to pay for the lights, much less everything else.

Let me say it again: If you did nothing else but play the pass line with odds, you'd be a relatively successful craps player (and by successful, I mean that you'd lose a lot less than everyone else). But if you want to take your game up a notch into a riskier, albeit potentially more lucrative, area, you'll need to learn a few more tricks.

COME BETS

Come bets are essentially a come-out roll after the point has already been made. So say you're the shooter and you roll a 6, making the point a 6. But some people aren't happy with just one point number; they want action on more numbers, so they place another bet in the giant box marked "come." This is just another come-out pass-line bet, but it's made in the middle of a shooter's roll. So if the very next number is a 7 or 11, they automatically win their come bet (though of course they lose their original pass-line bet). If the shooter rolls a 2, 3, or 12 craps, the come bet loses, though nothing happens to their original pass-line bet. If the shooter rolls a point number like a 5, the come bet "travels" to the 5, and now that person has action on both the 5 and the 6. If either of those numbers repeats, he wins. Of course, if a 7 should rear its ugly head, he loses both bets.

Even better, once the come bet has traveled, the bettor can place odds on that bet as well, just like the pass line. He can even place another come bet so that he can have as many as six numbers working at any one time. Now this is wonderful when you've got those rare hot shooters who keep banging out point numbers. But it can be dangerous, because a single 7 can wipe out all your bets. So most pass-line bettors go with three numbers at the most and hope their numbers hit.

TALES FROM THE DARK SIDE

At some point you may have said to yourself, "If 7 is so powerful, why not just bet 7?" You can do exactly that by betting the complete opposite of the pass-line bettors. Instead of betting the pass line, you bet the don't-pass line. Instead of betting on the come, you bet on the don't come. And instead of cursing your luck when a 7 rolls, you simply take your winnings down.

Ah, but there's a catch. When you bet the don't-pass on the come-out roll, you lose when a 7 or 11 rolls but win when a 3 rolls (you will also lose with either a 2 or a 12; the number varies by casino). Once a point has been established, you're now rooting for the 7 to appear. However, you are rooting quietly, as almost everyone else looks with disdain on wrong-way bettors. The pass-line players are called right-way bettors, but don't be fooled—they're simply mirror opposites of each other. In fact, betting the don't pass has an ever so slightly lower house edge—1.36 percent—than betting the pass line.

Dark-side players also get free odds, though it's called laying odds instead of taking odds. The odds are definitely with you because the 7 is the number most likely to roll, so to counter the edge, you have to lay considerably more money down to win the same amount as you would if you were taking odds. For example, if the point is 4, instead of taking odds and winning $10 for every $5 you bet, laying odds sees you winning just the opposite: $5 for every $10 you bet.

The payout is structured that way because you have a huge advantage once the point is made—the probability of hitting 7 is on your side. If you're serious about squeezing craps for all it's got, and you have the bankroll to handle it, the wrong way is the best way of betting.

EVERY BET IN ITS PLACE

The only other bets I'm going to talk about in detail are the place bets, and that's because they're the only other semidecent bet on the table. And even then, not all place bets are good bets.

Suppose you don't want to go through the whole hassle of the come-out roll; you just want to bet certain point numbers (4, 5, 6, 8, 9, and 10). You can do that by merely making a place bet on your favorite number. After the come-out roll (though you can do it before, if you like), you toss the dealer some chips and tell him you want to place the 4 or the 5 or the 6 or the 8 or the 9 or the 10. There are advantages to making a place bet:

- Your number has to be rolled only once to get paid, not twice like a point number (once to establish the point and again to win).
- You can pick whichever number you want, such as 6 or 8, which have a much higher chance of appearing than 4 or 10.
- Instead of getting paid even money, as in a pass-line bet, a place bet gets paid slightly better, though not true odds.

# Bet	Pays	Example	House Edge
4 or 10	9 to 5	$5 bet is paid $9	6.7%
5 or 9	7 to 5	$5 bet is paid $7	4%
6 or 8	7 to 6	$6 bet is paid $7	1.5%

So if you bet $6 on the 6, you would get paid $7 when it's rolled (since the payoffs are 7 to 6, placing the 6 or 8 should be done in increments of $6 to get the most for your money; every other number can be bet in $5 increments).

However, there are cons to place betting as well:

- A pass-line bet wins if a 7 rolls on the come out. With a place bet, the 7 is always your enemy.
- You can't take free odds with a place bet, so the house edge is higher.

THE 6 AND THE 8

After all that I've said and done, the only place betting I can recommend is either the 6 or the 8 or, better yet, both at the same time. Either one comes up nearly as often as the 7, and when you bet both, you now have ten ways to win versus six ways to lose. Just be sure to stay away from a bet called the big 6 and 8. It's a bet in the lower corner of the craps layout, within easy reach of players (all the more to sucker you in with). This pays even money for the 6 or 8, and this is a horrible return on your investment. If you're going to bet the 6 and 8, get as much as you can and place bet them, even if you have to bother the dealer to do so.

🪙 THE REST OF THE WORST

Here's a list of the other craps bets you see on the layout. In almost every case, they're horrible, horrible, horrible opportunities that should be avoided at all costs.

The only reason I mention them here is to satisfy your morbid curiosity. Be warned, people who place good money on these bets will most certainly go broke.

FIELD BET

Above the come bet, you'll see a giant rectangle for the field bet. This one-roll bet (which means it's good for only the very next roll) will win if a 3, 4, 9, 10, or 11 is rolled. On most tables, a 2 pays double and 12 pays triple (or sometimes vice versa, depending on the casino). Sure, it sounds good, since you can win with seven numbers and lose with only four numbers. But look at the dice chart on page 87. The odds of rolling a field number are 16 to 36, whereas the odds of rolling a losing number are 20 to 36! This is what most people would call a sucker bet, though there is the rare occasion that it can be used profitably (see Strategy 3 at the end of this chapter). Otherwise, stay away.

PROPOSITION BETS

These bets are located in the center of the layout; they can be bet for the next roll of the dice at any time, and they carry a huge house edge (though just how big varies from casino to casino). Never, ever bet them. If you do, you may as well take this book and throw it in the fire, because you obviously haven't listened to a word I've said. To see why they're such bad bets, just consult the dice chart earlier in this chapter to see what the true odds of rolling these numbers are versus what you're getting paid.

Any Craps (2, 3, or 12)	Pays 7 to 1
Any 7	Pays 4 to 1
11	Pays 15 to 1
Ace-Deuce (1 and 2)	Pays 15 to 1
Aces (1 and 1)	Pays 30 to 1
12	Pays 30 to 1

"FOR" VS. "TO"

Which pays better: "8 for 1" or "7 to 1"? Believe it or not, as far as casinos are concerned, they pay exactly the same. It's just another trick the house uses to make you think something pays better than it really does. If a bet pays eight for one, the casino is saying, "we'll take your one unit, but in return I'll give you eight units back," leaving you with only seven more units then you started with. When it says seven to one, you know exactly what they're going to push across the table: seven units without touching your original one-unit bet.

HARDWAYS

These bets win if 4, 6, 8, or 10 are thrown in pairs, as pictured on the table layout. They lose when the number rolls "easy" (not in pairs) or if a 7 rolls first. The bets stay up until one of those three decisions are made or until you tell the dealer to take them off.

Number	Pays	Example	House Edge
4 or 10	7 to 1	$5 bet wins $40	11.1%
6 or 8	9 to 1	$5 bet pays $50	9.09%

PLAN OF ATTACK

In the world of craps, there are two methods that people choose to use when attacking the casinos: dice control (or as it's sometimes called, rhythmic rolling) or your usual trend-based system.

DICE CONTROL

Discussed in hushed whispers among the craps cognoscenti is the supposed phenomenon of dice control. Believers tell others that the key is to "set" the dice in a particular orientation, then throw them in such a manner that they don't tumble randomly. The theory is that by doing so, one or both of the dice will be more likely to show certain numbers.

Unlike other systems, this one is not mathematically absurd, because if it were possible to alter the probabilities of each outcome, then winning systems could be devised. Nevertheless, the casinos take steps to prevent this. The dice are supposed to hit the back wall of the table, which makes controlled spins more difficult. Whether it's possible for mere mortals to exercise the perfect precision one would need is pretty controversial, but there are some who swear by it.

As it stands, I think the jury is still out. I haven't seen any conclusive evidence proving it. I'm not saying that those who buy their own tables and practice 12 hours a day can't possibly get a favorable decision once in awhile. But as a system, it's comparable to card counting; most who claim they can do it are full of crapola.

 TREND SYSTEMS

A far easier method of attack is to merely exploit trends that are always coming along. There are only three types of trends at craps tables: hot, cold, and choppy.

- **Hot table:** At hot tables, shooters are banging off a lot of numbers—except for 7s.
- **Cold table:** Just the opposite. A shooter will establish a point and the 7 out.
- **Choppy table:** Not hot or cold. A shooter will establish a point and half the time roll the point again, or 7 out, but no clear trend is developing. Best to avoid these at all costs.

If you're playing the right side (that is, with the dice), you need to find a relatively hot table. Start by looking for crowded, noisy tables where there seems to be a lot of action, people are hollering, and point numbers are hitting. If the crowd is sparse, the people look glum, and all the bets being made are on the don't-pass line, this isn't the table for you. Of course, things can change in a moment, so be prepared to jump in and take advantage of a warm to hot table.

STRATEGY 1: "THREE-POINT MOLLY"

This is the most basic of craps bets and, mathematically speaking, the best one to make. Of course, it won't work at a choppy or a cold table. So use it only if it's a warm or hot table.

First you make a pass-line bet. Once the point is established, you back up your pass-line bet with full odds and at the same time make a come-line bet. Back up each come bet with full odds. Eventually you'll have three numbers working. If the table is hot, "press" each bet—that is, take your profits but let one additional unit ride on the bet. If the table is just warm, take down your bets each time it hits. This is the best way to take advantage of a hot trend and the only way to make a ton of money at the craps table.

STRATEGY 2: CLASSIC REGRESSION

In this strategy, you wait until the shooter has established a point before placing your bets. After the point is made, you'll place two units of $12 on both the 6 and 8. After one hit, you'll ask the dealer to come down one unit on both the 6 and 8.

Results: You now have a $2 profit and can no longer get hurt by the 7. In addition, you now have $12 working for you. After another hit, bring down all bets and wait for the roller to make his point or 7 out, then start the process over.

On two hits, your net profit is $21. Depending on how confident you are, you can come down after the first hit, profiting $14, or keep betting on the 6 and 8. If you prefer to keep your bets riding, make sure that both the 6 and 8 are covered.

STRATEGY 3: ANYTHING BUT 7

With this bet, you win when any number but seven is thrown. First off, wait until the shooter has established a point. Then place two units on the 5, 6, and 8 and then place one unit on the field. If a 5, 6, or 8 is rolled, you lose one unit in the field, but win two units from your place number.

This method is a little riskier than the previous strategies since your total monetary risk is $39. Therefore, I recommend you take your bets down after two rolls (three rolls at the absolute most, but only at a warm to hot table). Should the shooter hold the dice for at least three rolls, you will stand to win anything from $15 to $27 (more if the numbers 2 or 12 are rolled). After two or three rolls, take down all your bets and wait for the shooter to make either his point or 7 out.

Despite its Chinese name, pai gow poker (which rhymes with "high cow smoker") was invented by a couple Americans in the early 1980s in hopes of bringing more business to their California card room. Based very loosely on a Chinese domino game, pai gow poker uses a standard 52-card deck plus a joker. When playing in a casino, you're obviously playing against the house; when you play it in regular card clubs, you're playing one-on-one against an individual banker or a "corporation" who's there to back the action.

Pai Gow Poker

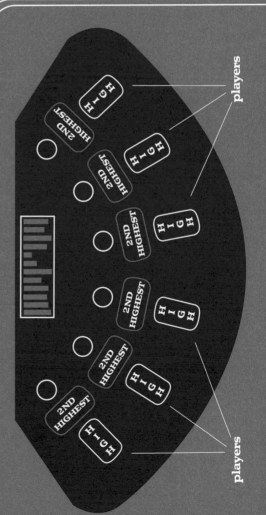

PAI GOW POKER TABLE

players

players

2ND HIGHEST

HIGH

After placing bets, everyone, including the dealer, gets seven cards dealt face down. Who gets the first set of cards is determined not by where you sit but by either a shake of the dice or a random number that's digitally displayed at the table. Then everybody arranges their cards into two separate hands, one with five cards (the high hand) and one with two cards (the low hand). Using typical poker ranks of hands, you make the best five-card hand you can with the cards you have. With your low hand, you try to make the second-best hand possible, which will be either a pair or two high cards.

For example, if you were dealt the Five of Spades, Five of Hearts, Six of Clubs, Seven of Diamonds, Eight of Clubs, Nine of Hearts, and Ten of Spades, you would put the straight (Six through Ten) in your five-card high hand, and put the pair of Fives in your two-card low hand. Here, the way you set up your hand is pretty obvious, but that's not always the case.

The Joker is "sorta wild" in that it can only be used to fill in straights or flushes, and if that doesn't work, it counts as an Ace. So in the above example, if you'd been dealt a Joker instead of the Eight of Clubs, you would have used it to fill in your straight.

Another thing to keep in mind is that your five-card hand must be higher than your two-card hand. Otherwise you "foul" and lose your wager. But the great part is, if you have any doubts or questions whatsoever, you can simply ask the dealer for help, and he'll make sure you don't foul and probably tell you how the casino would play your hand.

After everyone is done setting their hand, the dealer turns over his cards and sets his hand based on the house way, which is a set of rules that govern exactly how every dealer must set their hand in every possible situation, no exceptions.

Once that's done, he'll turn over each player's hand in turn and compare their low hand with his low hand and their high hand with his high hand. If the dealer's low hand beats the player's low hand and the dealer's high hand beats the player's high hand, the dealer wins, but he has to beat both hands before he can take the money. If he beats the low hand but loses against the high hand (or vice versa), it's a push, and the player keeps his money. If the dealer loses both the low hand and the high hand, then the player wins. There are a lot of pushes in Pai Gow Poker, as well as a low house edge of around two percent. So if you want a fairly slow-paced game that won't easily break your bankroll, this is the game for you.

PAYING TO WIN

Unfortunately, when a player wins, he doesn't get paid even money. There's a five percent commission taken out of your winnings, so if you bet $20 and win, you'll get paid $19. Why? Because the house has to make money some- how. Being roughly an even game, with both the dealer and the player likely to win, one of the only ways the house can make money is by charging a commission. That's why you want to bet in even $5 increments. If you bet odd amounts, the casino will round your bet up when calculating how much commission to charge. So if you bet $26 instead of $25, your commission would be $1.50, as if you bet $30, instead of the $1.25 that would be charged if you'd only bet $25. It might not seem like a lot, but I assume you are reading this book to cut as many costs as you can.

SQUEEZING JUST A BIT MORE

Another way that the casino gains an ever-so-small edge is by having ties go to the house. So if your low hand is an Ace and a King, and the dealer's low hand is also an Ace and a King, it's called a copy hand and the dealer wins the low hand, though he still has to win the high hand to take your money. The same is true if he has the same ranking of cards in his high hand; the tie goes to the house.

BANKING

The one big advantage in pai gow poker is that players can get a turn to act as the house by "banking." Now you get to win on ties! But when a player decides to bank, he must be able to cover not only his own bet, but the bets of everyone else at the table. This is great if only one or two people are playing, but it can be expensive if the table is full of $100 bettors. Worse, if you do win other players' money, the casino is still going to take five percent commission for their troubles. Nevertheless, when you consider that you have a slight edge against other players because of your ability to win ties, banking is a good idea if you can afford it. It's even better when you're going one-on-one with the casino. Not only do you get to bank more, but you don't have to feel guilty for taking your fellow players' money.

HOUSE WAY

To calculate and print out the absolute best way to play each and every hand would take pages and pages, so every casino has a shortened cheat sheet that dealers must memorize or consult that tells them how to play each and every hand. No house way is absolutely perfect, but they get awfully close. You could do far, far worse than to let the dealer set your hand for you and simply place your bet or take your winnings. In fact, most decisions, as in the previous example, are pretty clear-cut.

Memorize this particular house way, which is rather obvious except for the rarest of occasions. If you can't print it out or memorize it, then when you're faced with a tough decision, simply ask the dealer to set your hand the house way.

Your Cards	House Way	
No Pair	Place the highest card in the five-card hand and the next two highest cards in the two-card hand.	
One Pair	Place the pair in the five-card hand and the next two highest cards in the two-card hand.	
Two Pairs	See two pairs section below.	
Three Pairs	Always play highest pair in two-card hand.	
Three of a Kind	• Always play three of a kind in five-card hand, except break up three aces. • Two three of a kinds—play the lowest three of a kind as the five-card hand and split the higher three of a kind.	
Straight	• Keep as the five-card hand. • Six-card straight—use the highest card in the two-card hand. • Five- or six-card straight with a pair—use pair as the two-card hand. • Straight with two pair—play the two-pair rule.	
Flush	• Keep as the five-card hand. • Six-card flush—use the highest card in the two-card hand. • Five- or six-card flush with a pair—use the pair as the two-card hand. • Flush with two pair—play the two-pair rule.	
Straight & a Flush	A flush and a straight with no pair—play the combination that results in the highest two-card hand.	

Your Cards	House Way

Full House

Split except with pair of Two's and an Ace/King can be played in two-card hand.

Four of a Kind

Play according to the rank of the four of a kind:
- Two through Six: Always keep together.
- Seven through Ten: Split unless a pair or ace and picture can be played in the two-card hand.
- Jack through King: Split unless hand also contains a pair of Tens or higher.
- Aces: Split unless a pair of Sevens or higher can be played in two-card hand.

Straight Flush

- Keep as the five-card hand.
- Split two pair Tens and higher, or a pair of Aces and any other pair.
- Any other two pair with Ace—play the two pair as high and the Ace in the two-card hand.
- Play a straight or flush instead of the straight flush if it causes a picture card or higher to be played in the two-card hand.

Royal Flush

- Keep as the five-card hand.
- Royal flush with a pair—play the pair in the two-card hand.
- Royal flush with two pair—play the two-pair rule.
- Split the royal flush if an Ace, King, or a pair can be played in the two-card hand while retaining a straight or flush in the five-card hand.

Five Aces

Split unless pair of Kings can be played in two-card hand.

THE TWO-PAIR STRATEGY

While almost every pai gow decision is fairly obvious, the one that trips up most players and even some casinos is when to split your two pair and when to keep them together. The best method is to split your pair unless:

- The sum of the pairs equals 9 or less and you have a King or an Ace singleton, or
- The sum of the pairs equals 15 or less and you have an Ace singleton.

What do I mean by the "sum of the pairs"? Simple: Just take the ranks of each pair and add them up. So if you have a pair of Fours and a pair of Eights, you'd have a sum of 12. Face cards and Aces have the following value: Jack = 11, Queen = 12, King = 13, and Ace = 14.

SIDE (SUCKER) BETS

To make the game even more popular, many casinos offer it with various side bets and rename it something like "fortune pai gow." "For as little as a dollar" you can bet that you're going to get at least a straight or higher, with the jackpot being reportedly proportional to the rarity of your hand. So if you get a straight flush, you'll get paid 50 to 1, or something like that. Sounds good, but the odds are, naturally, stacked against you, and you'll rarely get anything that comes anywhere near to recovering the bets you've made.

PLAN OF ATTACK

Casinos typically charge 5 percent commission on your winning pai gow hands, but some will charge only 4 percent. In other words, if you win $100, some will charge you $5, and others will charge only $4. That may not seem like much, but when you're fighting for every penny against a ruthless foe, every dollar counts.

One casino I helped open didn't want to deal with quarters (and I mean the 25-cent coin, not $25 chips), so they did something almost unheard of: They rounded down. So if you bet $25, instead of charging you $1.25, you paid only a buck in commission. After playing a few hours, you could end up saving a couple of bucks, enough for the buffet.

Some card rooms will charge you a flat buck regardless of your bet, instead of the usual 5 percent commission. And if you bet more than $100, some card rooms waive the commission altogether. Naturally, it doesn't take an economics major to see the advantages here, as long as you're betting at least $25 or more.

 ## LOOK FOR A HAND-DEALT GAME

If you're planning to play pai gow poker, it's not because you plan on making a fast killing. You're probably wanting a slow-paced game with plenty of ties so that when you do lose, it'll be slow. Originally, pai gow poker had the dealer shuffling and creating seven equal stacks of seven cards, then rolling the dice to see who got the first stack of cards. Nowadays, a dealer just sticks the entire deck in a machine, and it quickly spits out the cards. Naturally, this speeds up the process (good for the house, bad for the player). If you're looking for a slow-paced game, look for casinos that still hand deal the game. There's even a belief that when a dealer hand deals the game, she doesn't shuffle the cards as thoroughly, so players will get better hands. I'm inclined to think this is garbage—but if it doesn't hurt you, why not?

FIND A COLD DEALER

As in the blackjack chapter, you're going to want to find a cold dealer, some-one who's doing nothing but giving money away. If he's standing by himself, you can simply ask if he's killing 'em or not. If all the tables have people at them, it's very easy to see if the dealer is going through a good trend or a bad trend by merely watching a few hands. When the dealer turns his hand over, is it a monster hand or is it easily beatable? Do the people at the table look happy or miserable?

Unlike blackjack, the other players won't worry about you ruining their winning streak when you sit down at their table—so they'll gladly tell you whether the dealer is on fire or not. They'll probably talk about it every time the dealer turns over his hand.

Yes, I know that thanks to the dice or the random number generator, the order of the cards changes every single hand, but that still doesn't change the fact that I've seen dealers continue to pound the players no matter what they did. You are merely trying to catch a lucky streak, so why lean into the punches if the dealer is doling them out? Just look for a friendlier table.

RIDE SOMEONE ELSE'S LUCK

If someone else at the table seems to be catching the monster hands and not you, many casinos will let you place a side bet on his spot if the player doesn't have a problem with it. Of course, you don't have any control over how the player chooses to play his hand—but that's a fair trade for piggy-backing on someone else's hot streak.

MONEY MANAGEMENT

As in every other table game, in pai gow poker you're going to use a progressive betting system, although you're not going to press your bets as rapidly as you did with blackjack. Also remember that you are getting dinged a 5 percent commision on every winning wager, so you're not quite winning even money on every bet.

 ## DON'T FORGET THE THREE-STRIKES RULE

If you've lost two hands in a row, it's time to seriously think about changing things up. If there's an extra open betting circle, you can go ahead and try those cards, or simply bet on another person's hand. But if you get that fateful third losing hand in a row, you must switch tables or at least take an extended break. Never continue betting when you're losing—that's what the casino wants you to do, and that's how you're going to destroy your bankroll. Go play another game, go take a nap, go eat some lunch, but in any case, don't continue playing at this table against this dealer.

WHEN A WINNING STREAK HAPPENS

Pai gow poker isn't really a game of streaks like blackjack or baccarat. It's usually a game of win a few, push a lot, lose a few. So pressing your bets isn't the best way to play. Here you'll actually want to use the New York progression as detailed in chapter 2's "Money Management" section (page 27). In a nutshell, start with two units, and with a win lower it to one unit then back up to two units. When winning, your progression will go 2, 1, 2, 3, 4, 5, and return back to two units on any loss.

BANKING

I've seen more profits lost from players banking than from anything else in pai gow poker. Most who decide to do so are on a horrible losing streak and are desperate to change things up. Unfortunately, they're counting on being able to go against the trend and scoop up everyone else's money in the process. Naturally, I strongly discourage you from banking if you're losing.

However, if you're on a nice winning streak and have made a bit of money, than go ahead and take a shot. Even better is if you're playing one-on-one with the dealer and can ideally bank every other hand. You have the advantage because ties now go to you instead of the house, so the more you can bank, the better. Unfortunately, good opportunities for banking are pretty rare, but they're worth the trouble if you can pull it off.

Ever wanted to bet big money on a coin flip? Are you looking for a game with a low house edge that's easy to play? Then step right up, and welcome to baccarat. The house edge on the best bet is only 1.06 percent, and playing is almost as simple as betting heads or tails.

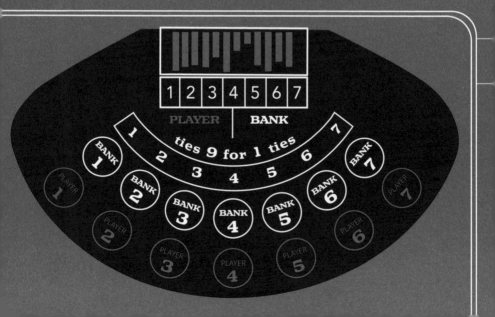

BIG BACCARAT TABLE

MINI BACCARAT TABLE

There are two types of baccarat (pronounced "baw-caw-rah"). First, there's big-table baccarat, which is sometimes just called bacc (pronounced "bawk"). There's also the much more common mini-baccarat (or mini-bacc), which is played on a much smaller table. The rules are exactly the same, but the snob factor is different for each.

MINI-BACCARAT

The table in mini-baccarat looks very much like a large blackjack table, and the dealer does all the work. All you have to do is bet heads or tails—er, I mean, player or banker. Those are your two choices. It's that simple.

THE RULES

Baccarat is played from a six-deck or an eight-deck shoe. All face cards and Tens have no value. Cards less than Ten are counted at face value, Aces are worth 1 and suits don't matter. Since the highest score is a 9, we ignore the left digit of any card total that is 10 or higher. So 15 is counted as 5, and 23 is counted as 3. A King and a Six count as 6, and a Nine and an Eight count as 7 (9 + 8 = 17, and then you lop off the left digit).

To start, the players place a bet on player, banker, or tie. The dealer will dole out two cards for each side, first to the player spot and then to the banker spot. He then turns over the cards to reveal the scores. The object of the game is to bet on the hand that you think will have the highest total value—you have roughly a 50-50 shot.

If the first two cards achieve a count of 8 or 9, it's called a natural and wins automatically (unless you get two naturals exactly tied; then it's a push). If neither hand is a natural, an additional third card may be dealt to the player, the banker, or both, depending on a series of relatively complicated rules that we will touch on in a moment. Don't worry, you don't need to learn or even know the rules; the casino dealer follows them whether you know them or not.

Another unique aspect of baccarat is if you bet on the banker and the banker wins, you'll be charged a 5 percent commission on your winnings. However, if you bet on the player and the player wins, there's no commission. You get paid even money.

This is because the banker is slightly more likely to win. So to even the odds a bit, the banker is charged a commission.

What's interesting, and what you won't learn from reading any standard baccarat strategy guide, is that even after the 5 percent house commission, there is still an advantage to betting on the banker. The margin is slim at 0.19 percent, but it does exist.

Ties

Besides player and banker, you can also bet on tie, which promises a payout of 8 to 1 if both hands end up being equal. While the payout might seem enticing, it's actually a sucker bet with a house edge of more than 14 percent, for the odds of getting a tie are closer to 10 to 1. Naturally, you should bother to play only if you're a sucker.

BIG-TABLE BACCARAT

Big-table baccarat is generally played in a roped-off area separate from the rest of the commoners—oops, I mean, other ordinary casino games. The players are generally as well-dressed as the tuxedo-clad dealers, and the table minimums are high.

The shoe rotates around the table, just like the dice at craps, giving each player a chance to deal the cards. And just as in craps, if a player doesn't want to deal, he or she can pass the shoe to the next player.

The player with the shoe acts as the dealer and as "banker," but this person doesn't actually bank the game. In fact, the "dealer-banker" (that is, the player who's controlling the shoe) can bet on player or banker (though typically they'll bet banker or otherwise pass the shoe), as the role of the banker is merely ceremonial.

The person who has bet the highest amount on the player is given the player cards and simply turns them over, announcing their total. The actual casino dealer then instructs the dealer-banker whether to draw a third card and then announces the winning hand. Finally, the actual casino dealers will pay the winners and collect the losers out of the casino dealer's tray.

As you might imagine, the game can go mind-numbingly slow compared to the relative speed of craps or blackjack. Some people like to take forever to turn over their player cards, and sometimes they bend the cards so much that they become permanently damaged. But that's okay; if you're betting $5,000 a hand, the casino can afford to replace each new shoe with brand new decks.

DRAWING RULES

• All bets are made before the cards are dealt.

• If either the player or the banker has a total of an 8 or a 9, they both stand. There are no exceptions, and this rule overrides all other rules.

• If the player has a total of 6 or 7, the player stands.

• If the player stands, the banker hits on a total of 5 or less.

• If the player has a total of 5 or less, the player automatically hits, and the banker gives the player a third card.

• If the player gets the third card, the banker draws a third card according to the following rules:

☆ **Banker has total of 0, 1, or 2:** Banker always draws a third card.

☆ **Banker has total of 3:** Banker draws if player's third card is 1-2-3-4-5-6-7-9-0 (not 8).

☆ **Banker has total of 4:** Banker draws if player's third card is 2-3-4-5-6-7.

☆ **Banker has total of 5:** Banker draws if player's third card is 4-5-6-7.

☆ **Banker has total of 6:** Banker draws if player's third card is of 6-7.

☆ **Banker has total of 7:** Banker always stands.

You can use the following table to determine whether the banker hits (H) or stands (S) if the player has drawn a card.

BANKER'S SCORE	PLAYER'S THIRD CARD									
	0	1	2	3	4	5	6	7	8	9
7	S	S	S	S	S	S	S	S	S	S
6	S	S	S	S	S	S	H	H	S	S
5	S	S	S	S	H	H	H	H	S	S
4	S	S	H	H	H	H	H	H	S	S
3	H	H	H	H	H	H	H	H	S	H
2	H	H	H	H	H	H	H	H	H	H
1	H	H	H	H	H	H	H	H	H	H
0	H	H	H	H	H	H	H	H	H	H

DEALER SHORTCUTS

No dealer who learns how to deal baccarat memorizes all these numbers; they just learn a couple of rules. As long as they keep these things in mind, they know exactly when to draw and when not to. You can learn these rules, too, so you can follow what the hell is going on:

• If either hand has an 8 or a 9, it's a natural and there are no draws, period.
• If the player has a 6 or a 7, there are no more draws for the player.
• If the player has a 5 or less, there is one card drawn for the player. Whether the dealer draws another card for the banker is all determined by what the banker has and the value of the card the player gets. But it all boils down to this:

☆ **38 Special:** This hand is special because if the banker has a total of 3, he'll draw on any player card except Eight.

☆ **Four 27:** If the banker has a total of 4, he'll draw a third card only if the player's third card is a Two through Seven.

☆ **Five 47:** If the banker has a total of 5, he'll draw a third card only if the player's third card is a Four through Seven.

☆ **Six 67:** If the banker has a total of 6, he'll draw a third card only if the Player's third card is a Six or a Seven.

PLAN OF ATTACK

Baccarat is most definitely a game of streaks. In fact, this is such common knowledge that casinos provide paper and pens to players so they can keep track of the streaks themselves (though some are starting to use electronic boards similar to the ones they have for roulette so you can easily see trends).

Of course, there's no way of knowing when a streak will begin or when it will end; just be prepared to take advantage of a streak when it happens. Following are the best methods for doing so.

FOLLOW THE BANK

Despite charging a 5 percent commission on every winning banker hand, betting banker is still a better bet. Banker wins, on average, five extra times a shoe. So for this method, merely wait for a banker decision to show and then start betting banker, using the 2-1-2 down and up progression.

FOLLOW THE SHOE

While banker is a slight favorite to win, I have seen huge streaks for player, sometimes more than 10 in a row, with streaks of six and seven being very common. Here, you simply bet two units on whatever won the last decision. If you win that one, you regress to one unit, then back up to two if you win that one as well. Then keep increasing your winning bets by one unit until you lose.

FOLLOW THE LUCK

There are times when, for whatever reason, someone at the table gets lucky. Either it's his lucky day, or he's using some secret card-counting method no one's ever heard of, or maybe he and the dealer are in cahoots. Whatever the reason, he seems to be winning a heckuva lot more than he's losing. If you happen to find someone like that, most casinos have no problem with you side betting on his spot. When he wins, you win. So strike while the iron is hot.

CASINO TRICKS

If the table seems to be losing a lot of money in a short time, there's not a whole lot a casino can do about it. It's not like they can change the dice or drop the shoe (at least, they're not supposed to). They can only speed up the game. If you notice that the pit boss is talking to the dealer, be sure that you place your bets as fast as you can because the casino may be trying to throw people off their rhythm.

CHAPTER 9

Games like blackjack, craps, and roulette have been around forever—and many casinos recognize that the MTV-loving, Playstation-playing generation of 20- and 30-somethings are looking for something new, some games to call their own. So they've invented a whole handful of new "carnival games," usually with obscenely high house edges, to satisfy the influx of new and naïve customers. In this chapter, we will discuss two of the most popular: three-card poker and let it ride.

Three-Card Poker and Let It Ride

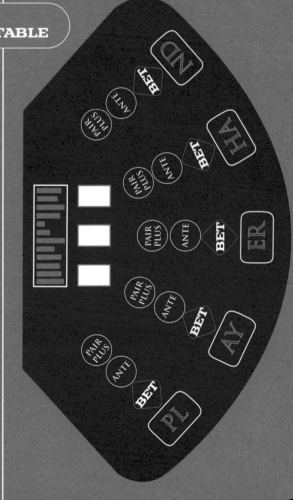

THREE-CARD POKER

Three-card poker is actually two games in one; players have the option to bet different amounts on either one or both. As the name implies, it is a poker-based game played with three cards, and three cards only. No draws.

The first game (the top circle) is called pairplus and is so named because you get paid whenever you have at least a pair in your hand. It doesn't matter what the dealer has because you're paid strictly on what sort of three-card hand you have. If you have a pair, you get paid even money. If you have a three-card straight or a three-card flush, you get paid even more (the amount varies by casino). And if you have three of a kind or, even better, a three-card straight flush, then you can really rack up the dough.

Sounds like a pretty sweet deal, and it was . . . when it first came out. Since three-card poker premiered in 1999, the once-generous pay tables have been scaled back, making the game less lucrative than it used to be. For example, players used to get 4 to 1 on a flush and 6 to 1 on a straight (with only three cards, it's actually harder to get a straight than a flush), which gave the house an edge of only 2.3 percent. Then someone got the bright idea to change a flush payout to 3 to 1. That one tiny change triples the house edge to 7.28 percent!

ANTE AND PLAY

The second game requires you to place a bet in the ante square before you get your cards. Once your hand is dealt, you can fold and lose your ante bet. Or, if you like what you see, you can match your ante bet with an equal bet in the play circle directly below it. Now the dealer turns over his poker hand and sees who has the higher hand.

QUALIFYING

In three-card poker, the dealer must "qualify," that is, he must have at least a Queen high in his hand. Of course, if he has a pair or better, it's a qualifying hand. But if he has something like Jack, Nine, Seven, the hand doesn't qualify. If the dealer doesn't qualify, it doesn't matter what you have in your hand—the dealer will pay even money for your ante bet but push your play bet.

If he does qualify, and your hand is higher, you'll get paid 1 to 1 on both your ante and your play bets. If you've got a really good hand, like a three of a kind or a straight flush, you'll get paid extra on your ante depending on the casino's bonus pay tables. If his hand is higher, you obviously lose both ante and play.

Interestingly, if you decided to stay in with lousy cards, it doesn't matter if the dealer's cards are higher than yours if he doesn't qualify; you still win the ante but push the play.

PLAN OF ATTACK

Obviously, you should try as hard as you can to scope out a casino that offers the most generous pay tables, that is, one that pays 4 to 1 on a flush and 6 to 1 on a straight. Yes, everyone's hoping to win the really big bonus of a straight flush, but you need to keep your bankroll going by being paid in full for all the straights and flushes you get.

Again, don't be shy to ask the dealer if he or she is playing hot. If the table has players, look at the cards being dealt. If all systems are go, sit down and start placing your bets.

Even though it's not the best of bets, you're definitely going to want to play both the pairplus and the ante portion of the game, otherwise, why play three-card poker at all? Don't play just the pairplus; it's the worse of the two bets. And don't just play the ante, because when you do finally get a three of a kind or straight flush, you'll be kicking yourself for not having played pairplus. Next, you want to take the same tactic as the dealer and keep hands that have at least a Queen or higher. Yes, sometimes it's tough when you have a

Queen-Seven-Five, but trust me, it's better than throwing your hand away. Just pray that the dealer doesn't qualify.

I've dealt to people who like to play "blind" and not look at their cards; they just match their ante bet automatically, hoping to win or, at worst, hoping the dealer doesn't qualify. I guess if you came to gamble, you indeed came to gamble, but this tactic is just dumb and will deplete any winnings much faster than playing according to the strategy described above.

MONEY MANAGEMENT

Three-card poker is unique because no matter what you have, if the dealer doesn't qualify, you'll still end up ahead on your ante wager. This usually ends up in a push, as most people bet one unit on pairplus, one unit on ante, and one unit on play. If you don't have at least a pair in your hand, you lose the pairplus, win one unit on ante, and push the play, for a net win of 0.

Therefore, the best way to play is to put one unit on pairplus (the worse of the two bets) and two units on the ante. That way, if the dealer doesn't qualify (which happens surprisingly often), you lose your pairplus bet but gain two units on your ante for a net win of one unit.

SAY IT WITH ME NOW: "THREE STRIKES AND YOU'RE—"
Outta there, right? If you lose your pairplus, ante, and play bets three times in a row, you have to get up and go to another table.

LET IT RIDE

Let it ride was invented in 1993 by Shuffle Master founder John Breeding, in hopes of spurring sales of the company's automatic shuffle machines. Second in popularity only to three-card poker, this "specialty" game definitely has its fans due to the fact that players are allowed to pull back a portion of the original bet *after* seeing their cards.

HOW TO PLAY

First you place three equal bets in the three spaces marked $, 2, and 1. So if you're betting $5, you'd place a total of $15 altogether, $5 on each spot. Each player then receives three cards face down while the dealer gets two cards face down. The dealer's cards function as "community cards" for the entire table; all the players will use them to try to make the best five-card hand.

You then look at your three cards, hoping to get at least a pair of Tens (the minimum hand that results in a payout) or better. If you don't like what you see, you can pull back one of your bets (the unit placed on the 1). The dealer then turns over the first community card. At this point, the players can analyze their hands and, if they like, take off another unit (the bet on the 2). The dealer turns over the second community card, and the player knows his total five cards. Anything from a pair of Tens up to a royal flush results in a win; payouts vary from casino to casino, but below is a sample pay table:

Hand	Payout
Royal Flush	1000-1
Straight Flush	200-1
Four of a Kind	50-1
Full House	11-1
Flush	8-1
Straight	5-1
Three of a Kind	3-1
Two Pairs	2-1
Pair of Tens or Better	1-1

If you are playing with optimum strategy, the house edge with the above table is 3.5 percent.

SUCKER SIDE BET

Naturally, let it ride has a bonus bet to get you to fork over just a little bit more money. And like most bonus bets, it's one of the worst opportunities in the game. This bonus usually pays off if you have two pair or better, again depending on the pay table at that particular casino. The house edge starts at more than 13 percent and can go as high as 35 percent if you're unfortunate enough to be playing at a real cutthroat casino. As usual, my advice is to avoid bonus bets like the plague.

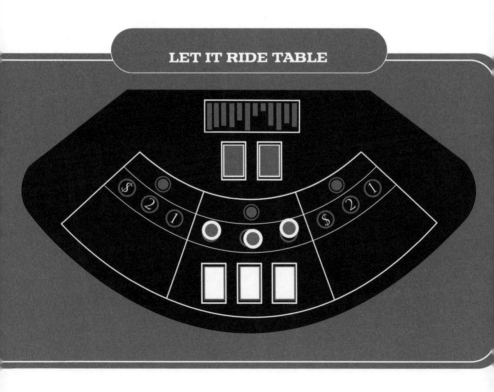

LET IT RIDE TABLE

PLAN OF ATTACK

If you must play this game, you need to avoid the temptation to let it ride whenever you're trying to get lucky. And follow my advice to cut the odds against you to the barest minimum:

You should pull back your first bet (1) unless you have one of the following:

- **A winning hand** (a pair of Tens or better)
- **Three cards to a royal flush**
- **A three-card straight flush** in which the lowest card is a Three or better

Notice that you do not let it ride if you simply have a three-card flush, such as Three-Six-Eight of Spades. The chances of getting a five-card flush are too small at this point to afford to gamble.

Once the dealer turns over his first community card, you should pull back your second bet (2) unless you have the following:

- **Any paying hand** (a pair of Tens or better)
- **Four to a flush**
- **Four to an open-ended straight.** For example, you have 4-5-6-7. There are eight cards that can make your straight, Threes and Eights, so it's worth the gamble.
- **Four to an inside straight**, if the four cards are Ten or higher. For example, you have Ten-Jack-Queen-Ace of mixed suits. You need a King to complete the straight, but you have four other cards that, if you pair them up, you still get paid, so it's worth the risk.

 MONEY MANAGEMENT

One would think it'd be pretty easy to get at least a pair of Tens, but anyone who has played let it ride knows that it's actually pretty tough.

When you decide to play, try to find a casino that offers the most generous pay table, which is the one shown on page 125. Then scope out a table that looks as if the players are having lots of fun; the dealer's smiling, the players are happy and have plenty of chips. You're looking for a table that's on a positive trend.

With let it ride, the best money strategy is to merely flat bet whether you win or lose. Streaks are an enormous rarity, and considering that you're dealing with varying bets depending on when you stay or pull back, it's better just to keep it simple and flat bet.

With that being said, you must still absolutely follow the three-strikes rule: Lose three in a row and move to another table, another game, or another casino.

OTHER CARNIVAL GAMES

The two games described in this chapter have enjoyed enormous success, but the casinos have engineered many more. I can't recommend any of them. No caribbean stud, no big-six wheel, nothing else the casino dreams up to sucker you out of your money. Focus on the games with the lowest possible house edge. Compared to "traditional" casino table games like craps, blackjack, and baccarat, the house edge on three-card poker and let it ride is unusually high. And other carnival games are even worse. Consider:

• Caribbean Stud
In many ways similar to three-card poker, this game challenges you to match your five-card poker hand to the dealer's five-card poker hand. Even if you somehow mastered the rather complicated optimal strategy, you're still looking at a house edge of 5.224 percent.

But wait, there's more. The real reason people play this game is for the sucker side bet that promises to pay out an ever-increasing progressive jackpot if you're lucky enough to get a royal flush. The house edge on this bet (which is actually the driving force behind its popularity) averages 26.46 percent. If you're going to gamble like that, you might as well spend your money on slot machines.

• **Big Six Wheel**
This giant wheel of misfortune is one of the casino's biggest moneymakers. Much like those oversized upright carnival wheels you see at the fair, this one sports a countertop inlaid with bills of various denominations. Take your dollar bill and place it on the note you think the wheel will stop. Guess right and you get paid that amount: $1 for guessing the $1 bill, $20 (or 20 to 1) if you guessed the $20 bill. If you pick Joker or Logo, you get paid 40 to 1. Easy, right? Well, even the best bet ($1) has a house edge of 11.11 percent. If you want to guess the $20 bill, you're staring at a house edge of 22.22 percent! And it only gets worse. Stay away!

• **Any Other New Games the Casinos Dream Up to Sucker You Out of Your Money**
Ignore the fancy sales pitches. The casino wouldn't be offering it if it wasn't a sucker bet. Don't play it!

CHAPTER 10

Don't play it!

Keno is nothing more than a casino-sponsored lottery. It offers the worst odds in the house and absolutely no chance of winning a life-altering windfall.

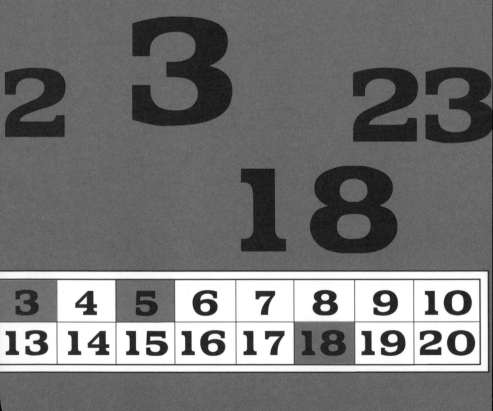

A Very Short Chapter on Keno

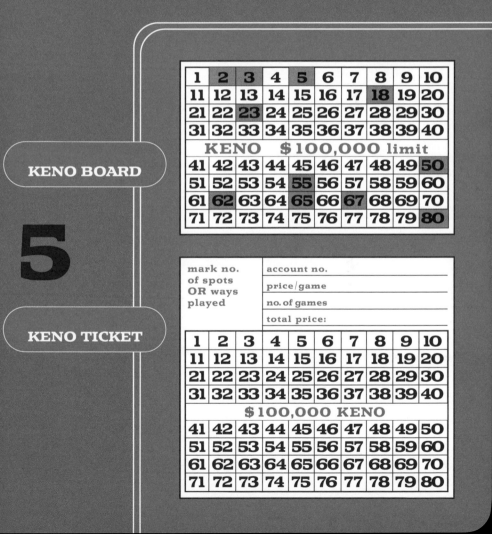

KENO BOARD

1	2	3	4	5	6	7	8	9	10
11	12	13	14	15	16	17	18	19	20
21	22	23	24	25	26	27	28	29	30
31	32	33	34	35	36	37	38	39	40

KENO $100,000 limit

41	42	43	44	45	46	47	48	49	50
51	52	53	54	55	56	57	58	59	60
61	62	63	64	65	66	67	68	69	70
71	72	73	74	75	76	77	78	79	80

5

KENO TICKET

mark no. of spots OR ways played	account no.
	price/game
	no. of games
	total price:

1	2	3	4	5	6	7	8	9	10
11	12	13	14	15	16	17	18	19	20
21	22	23	24	25	26	27	28	29	30
31	32	33	34	35	36	37	38	39	40

$100,000 KENO

41	42	43	44	45	46	47	48	49	50
51	52	53	54	55	56	57	58	59	60
61	62	63	64	65	66	67	68	69	70
71	72	73	74	75	76	77	78	79	80

There was a time when slot machines were simple babysitters for wives and girlfriends while the men went and played real games, like blackjack and poker. Nowadays, slot machines are the bread and butter of casinos. Anywhere from 70 to 85 percent of casino profits come from these simple one-armed bandits. Casinos absolutely love them. They never call in sick, and the overhead is minimal (especially when compared to table games). You just set them up and watch them bring in several hundred dollars a day, per machine, day in and day out.

What's not to like?

SLOT MACHINE

HOW SLOT MACHINES WORK

Contrary to rumors, superstitions, and casino urban legends, modern-day slot machines are pretty simple. In a three-reel game, a random number generator (RNG) picks three random numbers as soon as you press spin (or pull the lever). Then the machine spins the reels so that they stop on the spots selected by the RNG. It's the same for five-line video slots: five random numbers, one for each reel.

Sharp readers will notice that by the time the reels are spinning, the outcome has long since been decided. The whole spinning of the slots is merely to keep the player relatively entertained. It could just as easily be set up to say "Win" or "Lose" as soon as you press the button, but then the slot machine wouldn't be nearly as much fun.

THE RANDOM NUMBER GENERATOR (RNG)

Most players have a hard time accepting this, but the outcome on a slot machine is completely random. The RNG is always working, even when you aren't playing, picking thousands of three-number combinations per second. The moment you pull that lever or press the spin button, the RNG almost instantly determines the outcome.

Here's another way of understanding how a slot machine works. Imagine that the slot machine is a post office with 1,000 separate mail slots, each with its own envelope. Most of those envelopes are empty—they're losers. Some have a little bit of money, a few have a lot of money, and one has a big jackpot. When you pull the lever, the RNG picks one of those envelopes at random and simply displays the results via the reels (while the machine turns over the contents of the envelope, which is usually nothing). When a customer hits the button again, the RNG picks another random number, and game play continues. That's a gross oversimplification about what's happening, but you get the idea. Some machines have only a few hundred "envelopes" (or possible reel combinations), whereas others have thousands. But eventually, if it gets played enough, the RNG will eventually go through all the combinations at least once.

The most common misconception about slot machines always surfaces when someone hits it big on a machine that another person has just abandoned. The previous player always says, "I was just playing that machine! I should've played it a little longer, and I would've hit!" Although this is possible, it's pretty unlikely. Remember, the RNG is constantly selecting thousands of different combinations per second. So unless you pressed the spin button at precisely the same split-second as the other person, you wouldn't have won.

SLOT RETURNS AND PAYBACKS

When a casino slot manager orders a new machine, he or she has to make three decisions—the theme (I've seen everything from *Wheel of Fortune* to Elvis to *Star Trek*), the denomination (pennies, nickels, quarters, etc.), and the payback. He or she puts in an order, and the machine arrives preprogrammed to these specifications.

Depending on the jurisdiction, slot machines can pay back anywhere from 85 to 100 percent (and in very, very rare cases, more) of every dollar wagered. So if a slot machine is set to pay back 93 percent, that means that for every $100 fed into it, it will return $93 . . . over the next 10 million slot pulls. Naturally you can't expect to put in $100 and have it give you exactly $93. Sometimes you'll wager several hundred dollars before you get any money back, and sometimes customers put in $20 and hit a big jackpot right away. But over the course of a year, when the numbers are analyzed, it will even out to be about $93 for every $100 put through the machine.

LOOSE AND TIGHT
Customers (and many casinos) like to describe slot machines as either "loose" or "tight," when what they're really saying (without realizing it) is that a

machine's payback percentage is relatively high ("loose") or relatively low ("tight"). A machine's payback percentage will depend on the casino, where it's located, and the denomination of the machine. Every state-regulated casino has strict limits regulating how little a slot machine can pay out—but nearly every casino has their machines set to pay back more than the state minimum. For example, the minimum payback required by law in Nevada is 75 percent, but almost all machines in that state pay back at least 90 percent, and it's easy to find 95 percent. In Atlantic City, the state requires the lowest payback to be 83 percent, but again, you'll rarely find a machine that pays less than 90 percent.

So how do you find out how tight or loose the machines are at a particular casino? Well, it helps if you're sleeping with the slot manager, but there are other ways. Many states, like Colorado, require casinos to report the slot percentages, some broken down by denomination. A visit to the state's gaming control board (or the board's Web site) can usually produce the info you seek. And magazines devoted to slots also regularly publish slot machine paybacks for areas around the country.

The Competition

Obviously, the more competition a casino has for business, the looser their machines are going to be. The slot manager isn't going to order a bunch of low payback machines if there are five other casinos within a short driving distance. Players will notice and won't come back. Naturally, this means that places like Vegas, Reno, and other high-concentration gambling areas will generally have better-paying slots, whereas remote, out-of-the-way Podunk casinos will have machines that pay out much less—within reason, of course. If the slot machines are too tight, players just won't bother to show up.

Penny Machines: Paying for the Entertainment

Slot machines cost money, whether it's the cost of renting them, the electricity required to run them, or the cost of maintaining them. And of course the casinos would like to make a small profit from them. It goes without saying that a customer has to push a lot of pennies into a slot machine for a casino to make any money from it. As the denominations go up—nickels, quarters, dollars, five dollars, and more—the payback percentage can be higher for the customer because the casino doesn't need to keep as much to be profitable. As one slot manager told me, "If you're going to play penny machines, you're going to pay for the entertainment."

Also, when a casino orders their machines, they'll order the same payback percentage for each of their denominations. So if a slot manager wants a nickel machine to pay back 92.5 percent, all nickel machines will be 92.5 percent. It's a rare casino that mixes the same denominations with different paybacks.

SLOT MYTH-INFORMATION

Even the most well-educated people hold superstitious beliefs about slots. Keep in mind that slot machines are simply dumb computers—and as long as they're treated as such, you won't be bamboozled by the same misinformation.

CASINOS TIGHTEN SLOT MACHINES ON THE WEEKENDS

This is the most common variation of the most persistent myth around. I've even heard some customers insist that people in surveillance scope out the casino and pick one lucky customer, press a magic button, and make that customer's machine start winning. Another belief is that casinos can simply tighten or loosen a machine at will, as if there's some sort of handle on the back that the staff winds up on weekends and unwinds once the crowds have left. If you actually believed this, why on earth would you come to a casino? Trust me: Slot machines come preprogrammed to be as loose or tight as the casino wants. To change the payback percentage, you need to order a whole new computer chip (and sometimes a whole new computer board), then contact the appropriate regulatory authorities (so they can monitor your staff) as you open up the machine and change the hardware during several hours. It's such a hassle that most slot managers won't bother; it's easier just to order new machines.

 ## PULLING THE LEVER PAYS BETTER

In the early days, all slot machines had levers because they were purely mechanical. Today, everything is done through the machine's computer, so it makes no difference whether you pull the handle or press the spin button. In fact, both parts are wired to the same circuit. The only reason they still have levers is tradition, and there are still plenty of customers who prefer the feel of the pull.

 ## THE MACHINE'S LOCATION MAKES A DIFFERENCE

There was a time (back when all slot machines were boring three-wheeled cherries, lemons, and candy bars) when casinos would put the loose machines by the door and other high-traffic areas. Some authors have even perpetuated that myth today; if that's still the case, it's a rare exception and most definitely not the rule. With all the fancy bells and whistles and bonus games and video playback etc., etc., etc., people will play slots pretty much no matter where you put them. A slot manager these days is most concerned with aesthetics—having the layout of the slot floor look good, having the machines easily accessible, and putting machines where people will want to play them.

Far more important in slot payback is the denomination: Dollars pay better than quarters, which pay better than nickels, which pay much better than pennies.

THE AMOUNT OF TIME FROM THE LAST JACKPOT MAKES A DIFFERENCE

It's true that some machines seem to be just paying out like there's no tomorrow, or as some say, "on a pay cycle." However, there's no computer program that prevents or promotes a slot machine from paying more or less than normal. If it just hit a big jackpot, it's just as likely to hit (or not hit) again on the very next pull. These decisions are made by the random number generator; they are random.

In the casino where I'm currently working, we just installed a slot machine whose jackpot is supposed to be hit only once every 100,000 pulls, on average. But this machine hit three times before it went through its first 50,000 pulls. You just never know.

CASINOS PENALIZE PLAYERS WHO USE THEIR SLOT-CLUB CARDS

What possible reason would the casino have to punish you for inserting your slot-club card? Even in my most paranoid moments, I can't think of any reason. The slot-card equipment is not connected to the hardware of the slot machine; all it does is keep track of your play so you can earn the proper credit. Casinos want the customers to win sometimes; otherwise they won't come back and neither will their friends.

PLAYING "MAXIMUM BET" RESULTS IN MORE WINS

I've heard countless tales of people who play their machine with a maximum bet, but when their credits run low they drop their bet down and almost immediately hit the (now much smaller) jackpot. It's purely coincidence, and they forget all those times that they dropped their bet down and nothing happened. That's why I recommend always playing the maximum bet you can comfortably afford. No, it doesn't affect the odds one way or another. But you don't want to be kicking yourself if the jackpot hits.

PLAN OF ATTACK

Keep in mind that there are professional poker players and professional black-jack players, but there are no professional slot machine players. The system is so well designed by the casino industry that to win consistently is downright impossible. It's a helluva lot harder to find and exploit trends, as there's no way of knowing just by looking at a machine what kind of payback it has. But to increase the odds of getting lucky, go with these tips:

- **Play where there are lots of other casinos.** If they're the only game in town, what are the odds they're going to have loose slot machines? Competition means that casinos must have machines that pay high enough to keep people from going next door. So stick with Vegas, Reno, Atlantic City, and other popular places with several nearby casinos.
- **Stick with casinos, not airports.** In places like Nevada, you'll find slot machines at the airport and at every store. These machines are infamous for being tight *to the extreme.*
- **Go with the highest denomination you can afford.** If you can afford dollars but are playing pennies, then you're ruining your chances of winning. The higher the denomination, the higher the return. Of course, that doesn't mean you should play $25 slot machines if you've got only a hundred bucks. Be reasonable.
- **Use your slot-club card whenever you play.** The bonuses that you can get with your slot card include cash back, free meals, discounts at the gift shop, and even invitations to special casino events.
- **Keep in mind that progressive slots have less frequent payouts,** both big and small. You're going for life-changing money when you play progressives. If you want your money to last a bit longer with more frequent but smaller wins, then stick with the regular slot machines.

MONEY MANAGEMENT

You need to think hit and run, hit and run. If you plop yourself in front of one slot machine all day and continue to feed and feed and feed, you're going to go home broke, I guarantee it. So you need to pick a machine, give it a few pulls, take your winnings or lick your wounds, and move on.

After you've decided what slot machine you want to play, insert enough for twenty spins. If you're playing dollar machines, put in $20. Of course, if you are playing three credits per pull ($3), then you're going to need to put in $60. If you experience ten straight spins with not a single win, cash out and go to another machine. If you win-lose-win-lose but find you are down 50 percent of what you started with at that machine, again, cash out and find another machine. Don't play until you're out of money. Not only is it fiscally foolish, it's like a punch to the gut.

Look for banks of machines that proudly proclaim some high payback percentage, like 97 percent or more. But don't assume that the advertised high percentage applies to every machine. In all likelihood, it applies to only one machine in the bunch; the rest are probably closer to 90 percent. But you might as well try to get lucky there. Who knows? You could end up picking the higher-paying machine.

Back in the 1970s, a guy named Si Redd developed a new kind of slot machine based on the game of 52-card draw poker. His bosses at Bally wanted nothing to do with it, so he struck out on his own with his invention and founded the company that became IGT, creator of the most popular slot machines of all time. The video poker craze of the eighties and nineties had begun.

Unlike typical slot machines, video poker machines actually require some thought from the players, and devotees have all kinds of strategies. In fact, if players use a halfway-decent strategy, they can cut the house edge so much that video poker becomes one of the best bets in a casino.

Video Poker

VIDEO POKER

After inserting your money, you decide how many coins you're going to play per round. As with slots, bigger bets will result in bigger payouts, especially if you hit the video poker jackpot—the royal flush. Once you make your bet, push the deal button, and five cards are dealt to you face up. Sometimes you'll have an automatic winner, but usually you won't, and you'll have to decide which cards you want to keep (or hold) and which you want to discard.

Then you press the deal button and every card you've chosen to discard will be replaced with another card from the deck. Instead of beating another opponent's hand, you win whenever you have any five-card combination listed on the machine's payout table.

As with poker, video poker hands are valued based on their five-card ranking. These rankings are detailed below, 1 being the highest rank:

Rank Hand	Name	Description of Hand
1	Royal Flush	A, K, Q, J, 1 0 all of same suit
2	Straight Flush	Five cards of same suit in any sequence
3	Four of a Kind	Four cards of the same rank
4	Full House	Three cards of one rank, plus two pair of another
5	Flush	Five cards of the same suit
6	Straight	Five cards in sequence
7	Three of a Kind	Three cards of the same rank
8	Two Pairs	Two pairs of one rank, plus two of another
9	One Pair	Two cards of the same rank

JACKS OR BETTER

The original and still the most popular video poker game. To win, you have to have at least a pair of Jacks, and the payouts increase if your hand is better. No wild cards, no crazy variations, just straight, 52-card draw poker.

JOKER'S WILD

This game is much like your typical Jacks or better, but with a Joker thrown in as a wild card. This wild card can be used as a substitute for any other card or to create a five of a kind. The machine will automatically compute the best hand when a joker is present, and because of the added bonus of the wild card, the minimum rank for a winning hand is two pair.

DEUCES WILD

The standard 52-card deck is used, but all the Twos are wild cards. Naturally, that makes things more interesting (and easier to win), so the minimum winning hand is usually three of a kind.

BONUS POKER

Bonus poker is basically a variation of Jacks or better video poker with a higher-than-normal payout for a four of a kind and usually no wild cards. There are multiple versions of bonus poker with different "bonus" payouts for different types of four of a kinds.

DOUBLE DOUBLE BONUS VIDEO POKER

Double double bonus video poker pays off extra for paired hands. It is just an exaggerated version of double bonus video poker, which itself is a variation of the original Jacks or better game.

ALL THE OTHERS

New video poker variations seem to come out every week, but since the ones described on the preceding pages are the most popular, we'll concentrate on them.

PLAN OF ATTACK

After personal computers became as common as the microwave, it didn't take long for people to thoroughly analyze video poker machines. After all, the pay tables are printed right on the machine, and we know there are only 52 cards in a deck—so things like payback, house edge, and perfect strategy were worked out in short order.

There are countless video poker books detailing the absolute perfect play in every given situation for every single machine. Some gurus have devoted themselves to squeezing every last penny from their favorite machines and have found games that have a positive expectation. That means that with perfect play, the machine will theoretically pay out more than it takes in.

 FULL-PAY VIDEO POKER

Yes, you heard that right: With some video poker machines, you can get paybacks as high as 99.5 percent (Jacks or better) and even 100.76 percent (deuces wild). Video poker gurus scream from the rooftops that these low, low house edge machines, combined with slot-club player benefits such as cash back, free promotions, and two-for-one coupons, turned these narrow losers into narrow winners. Of course, these gurus have been screaming so loudly and so long that finding the "full pay" versions of these machines is getting harder and harder, even in cities like Vegas. And if you're outside Nevada—fuhgeddaboudit..

SOMETHING SMELLS ROTTEN

Gallons of ink have been spilled by video poker gaming gurus who claimed that serious players could actually *make* money from full-pay video poker machines. They had us believing that casinos were so generous and charitable that they'd kindly put these machines right out in plain view so that the smart player could easily turn a profit and help fund their retirement. There was only one problem: Corporations kept building more and more casinos, with nary a bankruptcy in the bunch. Some casinos even allowed these gaming gurus to hold special conferences with their guests to teach them how to beat the machines and the casinos.

Does that strike anyone else as odd?

While some cry grand conspiracy, methinks there are other reasons why the casinos haven't gone broke with their video poker machines.

- **Perfect strategy is tough.** To get your house edge so low on video poker, you have to play computer perfect. Sure, 95 percent of your play is pretty intuitive, but the other 5 percent starts to get a little tougher, with some minor nuances much harder to remember than basic blackjack strategy. Though the one or two mistakes you make may cost you only a few cents, they add up over time.

- **Players like to play.** When a guru hits a royal flush jackpot, he doesn't quit for the day and celebrate; he just keeps on playing. His followers naturally don't quit when they're ahead either, so they go through some pretty severe swings, sometimes where they win a bunch when they hit a royal, usually giving it all back before deciding to call it a day. But hey, they earned the free buffet that puts them theoretically in the black.

- **Casinos are getting smarter.** Now that everyone has heard that video poker can be beaten, the casinos are changing the payouts on the machines. Nothing major, just a few coins here and there to raise the house edge.

- **Playing video poker is work.** Most people play slots so they don't have to think. The strategy for video poker is so complicated that most devotees need to carry computer printouts detailing each and every move; most of the tourists you'll find in casinos are just looking to have a good time.

 STRATEGY

You're looking to have more than just a good time, of course, which means we need to teach you some basic VP strategy. I'm not going to insist that you learn every single detail. I see big video poker winners every day, and very few are playing perfect VP strategy. The fact is that if someone plays with a solid, intuitive strategy, they're surrendering only a percentage point or two to the house. What you're looking to do is hit one of the higher payouts and then quit for the day well ahead of the game.

If you do want to learn perfect VP strategy, by all means, don't let me stop you. But like card counting, I think you should do it as an intellectual exercise and not as a dogma. Learn it as a way of enhancing your playing experience, otherwise it becomes a drudgery.

JACKS OR BETTER

A full-pay Jacks machine is called a 9/6 Jacks or better machine, which means that it pays 9 coins for a full house and 6 coins for a flush. You can see this information right on the table at the top of the machine. Unfortunately, many casinos offer Jacks or better machines with payouts that are 8/5, 7/5, or 6/5. With each drop, the house edge goes up. So while the theoretical house edge on a 9/6 machine is only .48 percent, the house edges on the 8/5, 7/5, and 6/5 are 2.7 percent, 3.85 percent, and 5 percent.

You should try to find a full-pay Jacks or better machine (9/6) by carefully studying the pay tables. If you can't find one, you can drop down to 8/5, but only rarely should you go with a 7/5, 6/5, or one of those other ones that has some minor progressive for a royal flush payout. That's just throwing money away. Here's a simple strategy to help you in your play:

- **Never keep a kicker** (or extra card) in Jacks or better. Remember, you aren't playing against real opponents, so there will never be a need to "out-kick" your opponent with a high card. If you hold onto a pair, draw all three other cards to increase your chances of getting a three of a kind or a four of a kind.

- Never draw to an inside straight.
- Never keep three cards to a straight or three cards to a flush.
- Keep three cards to a straight flush if a potential royal flush is there, or if you don't have anything better to draw to.
- Keep two pair instead of trying to draw to four of a kind.
- Don't break a full house to try to get four of a kind.

DEUCES WILD

Four of a kind accounts for almost one-third of the payback percentage on a deuces wild game. So look for machines that offer at least a 5 for 1 payoff on a four of a kind. The other popular variation is affectionately called not-so-ugly deuces wild and only pays 4 for 1 on a four of a kind. It's called not-so-ugly because it actually pays out a bit better on a five of a kind and straight flush, though the change to the payout for four of a kind still raises the house edge. Never, ever play a deuces wild machine that pays less than 4 for 1 on a four of a kind. You'll just be throwing your money away. Here are a few more tips:

- Never hold a single card unless it's a deuce.
- Never discard a deuce, even if you have a draw to a natural royal flush.
- Never hold a deuce plus one card. The only time you should hold cards with a deuce is when you have more than one card to hold with it.
- Always keep a pair instead of drawing to get a flush or a straight.
- Never keep two pair. You must throw one of the two pairs away, and it doesn't matter which one.
- If you see a four of a kind less often than once every 10 hands or so, you're running cold and need to change machines.

MONEY MANAGEMENT

When you're playing video poker, you should manage your money much like you would for any other slot machine.

After you've found a video poker machine with the best possible pay tables, put in enough for 20 rounds. Remember that is going to be 20 rounds with full coins. So if you're playing a dollar machine with a full-coin payout that requires five coins, you're going to slide in a $100 bill. Now, if you experience ten straight spins with not a single win, cash out and go to another machine. If you win-lose-win-lose but find you're down 50 percent of what you started with at that machine, again, cash out and find another machine. Don't play the same machine until you're out of money. That's just stupid.

PLAY FULL COINS

As with slot machines, you need to play "max bet"—the full amount of coins you can wager on a single spin. Generally speaking, the difference between two through five coin payouts are simple multipliers of single coin payouts; sometimes the all-important royal pays significantly higher with full coins. And as I said in the slots chapter, you'll be kicking yourself if you get a four of a kind or better and get paid a quarter of what you would've been paid if you'd only bet more.

QUIT WHILE YOU'RE AHEAD

If you've hit enough high payout jackpots to double your initial money, get ready to quit. When you give back 20 percent, walk away from that machine. Go ahead and try another, but once you've given back half of your profits, quit your video poker playing for the day.

If, however, you've tripled or quadrupled or better by hitting a big payout, stop for the day. Sure, you can play a few more hands to see what happens, but don't give back more than your initial deposit. So if you put in $100 and hit for $1,000, don't give back more than $100. Stop for the day and enjoy your winnings. Buy something nice, something that you'll have to show for your good fortune.

I'm willing to bet that right after some caveman in the Stone Age invented gambling, some other caveman invented a gambling system. People have invested years of time and millions of dollars trying to beat any and all casino games. Every day I see people confidently marching into the casino with a sure-fire, can't-miss system that's certain to make them richer than Bill Gates. Some buy their systems off the Internet; others come with rules of their own creation. They always go on to break the bank and destroy every casino they set foot in.

I'm kidding! These people lose their money like all the other suckers.

OSCAR'S GRIND CHART

Bet and Outcome	Accumulated Loss/Win
Bet 1 unit and lose	-1 unit
Bet 1 unit and lose	-2 units
Bet 1 unit and lose	-3 units
Bet 1 unit and lose	-4 units
Bet 1 unit and win	-3 units
Bet 2 units and win	-1 unit
Bet 2 units and lose	-3 units
Bet 2 units and lose	-5 units
Bet 2 units and win	-3 units
Bet 3 units and win	0 units
Bet 1 unit and win	+1 unit

The series has been won

THE UNDENIABLE TRUTHS ABOUT GAMBLING SYSTEMS

In my years as a player, a dealer, and a pit boss, I've learned three things about gambling systems.

1. There are no new systems. Surf the Internet or (God forbid!) get on a gambling mailing list, and you'll read about thousands of systems for every-thing from blackjack to horse racing. But when you fork over your hard-earned cash for these secret systems, you receive the same tired old systems that have been floating around gambling circles since the invention of the wheel. Sure, some people have been able to put a little twist or two to the method, but the principles stay the same. And none of them work.

2. They all win (sometimes), and they all lose (eventually). As I've said before, people with far more brains, far more computing power, and far more time on their hands have all tackled these games. They've tried every system, method, and trick they can think of. And you know what? Sometimes the systems do work . . . for a while. But if you sit there at one table and continue to play, every system is going to fail—I absolutely guarantee it. There is just no way you can hope to plant your butt in one seat and overcome the in-evitable losing streaks.

3. Nobody believes me. Try as I might, despite my years of experience, when I tell people that gambling systems don't work, no one believes me. My friends will say, "But I was reading this brochure from a guy who promised that his system was completely different from anything that's ever been done before." And the next time I see that friend, he'll say, "You know what, you were right. That system I bought was complete BS." Even after reading this chapter, you're probably going to ignore my advice and try a few systems, maybe buy a few systems, and then lose a small fortune before you finally

come around and realize that no "mathematical" mechanical system will make you rich.

BEFORE YOU BUY A SYSTEM

I've seen systems advertised for peanuts and I've seen systems selling for thousands, all promising to turn your local casino into a bottomless pit of crisp hundred dollar bills. But I beg you, before you fork over any money—even if it's only $20—ask yourself these questions:

- If it's so good, why in the world would he sell it? Wouldn't he want to keep the "secret" to himself and not split any of the profits?
- How come you've never heard of him? If he was able to make such easy money, don't you think he'd be in *Time* magazine? Or at least the *Weekly World News*?
- If his method is so foolproof, why don't the casinos stop people from using it? Trust me: If there was an easy and profitable system for winning money at a casino, the casino would quickly come up with measures to stop it.

THE GRANDADDY OF THEM ALL: THE MARTINGALE

There is one system that every new player "invents" after he's played a while, but the system is older than you are. (Hell, it's even older than your grandparents.) It's the Martingale, or as others have called it, the double-up method.

The premise is simple: You merely double your bet after every loss, with the understanding that you can't keep losing forever. And when you finally win, you make up for all the losses so far. Sounds pretty good—in theory. When you actually have to put your cold hard cash out there, it's a totally different story.

For example, suppose you're going to bet red at the $1 roulette table. You lose the first spin, so you bet $2 on the next spin. You lose that one too, so you bet $4. You strangely lose that one as well, so now you're up to $8. You manage to win, and now you've recovered all of your losses, plus you're up a buck. Woohoo! You've just found the keys to the mint!

But not so fast. I've seen red miss 15 times in a row, and I've seen blackjack players lose more than ten hands in a row. What do your bets look like then?

Bet 1: $1	**Bet 5: $16**	**Bet 9: $256**
Bet 2: $2	**Bet 6: $32**	**Bet 10: $512**
Bet 3: $4	**Bet 7: $64**	**Bet 11: $1,024**
Bet 4: $8	**Bet 8: $128**	

Now you've lost only ten decisions in a row but more than $2,000 . . . all for a measly buck! Stop and think about it: Do you have the cojones to actually place a bet for $500 in the hopes of winning just $1?

More importantly, the casinos are wise to your tricks. Every table has betting limits that prevent you from continuing your progression much past 8. If it's a $1 minimum table, the maximum will probably be about $200, and there's no way it's going to be more than $500, much less $1,000.

If you think you can't lose more than a few hands in a row, think again. Sure, you may enjoy a few small wins. But eventually you'll hit a losing streak that will wipe out all of your profits.

Trust me: No one ever, ever, ever wins with the Martingale.

TYPES OF SYSTEMS

There are thousands upon thousands of systems out there, and they all boil down to two types: negative progressions and positive progressions.

NEGATIVE PROGRESSIONS

These systems are designed for you to recover your losses by increasing your bet after a loss. The Martingale is a perfect example, and it has hundreds of variations. These painful methods force you to try to go against the trend through sheer force of will and bet more when you're losing. All will have the same devastating impact on your bankroll.

POSITIVE PROGRESSIONS

Here you increase your bet when you're winning, in the hope of cashing in on a winning streak. This obviously makes more fiscal sense than negative progressions. But if you're stuck at a losing table, your few wins won't make up for your many losses.

THE CLASSICS

These systems have been around forever and continue to rear their heads every other week to take advantage of the constant influx of new, ignorant players. On the positive side, they've hung around because they actually are the best of the worst, the lesser of numerous evils. But if you insist on playing them mindlessly, like a robot, you are guaranteed to suffer small or even catastrophic losses.

THE GRAND MARTINGALE

If you thought the Martingale was bad, get a load of this: The Grand Martingale makes things even worse by trying to recover your losses . . . and then some. Instead of merely doubling your losing bet, you bet slightly higher so that when you do win, you get all your money back plus a few bucks for your troubles.

D'ALEMBERT

Supposedly invented by a Frenchman named Jean le Rond d'Alembert in the 1700s, this theory on the law of equilibrium proposes that for every loss there must be an equal number of wins. If red comes up 100 times, black must eventually come up 100 times as well. So what do you do? Simple, you just increase your bet by one unit after you lose and decrease your bet by one unit when you win, until you get back to your original starting bet. At that point, you simply continue to bet one unit until you lose.

For example: You start off betting $5. You lose, so you increase your bet by $5 and make your second bet $10. You lose that one as well, so your next bet increases by one unit to $15. You win, so you lower your next bet by one unit to $10. Unfortunately, you lose again, and you're back up to $15. Again you lose, so now your next bet is $20. You finally win and go back down to $15. The major fault with this system is that you can quickly get yourself in a hole, and when you finally do catch that winning streak, you aren't taking advantage of it because you're lowering your bet with each win.

CONTRA D'ALEMBERT

As the name suggests, it's just the opposite of the d'Alembert; you increase your bets one unit when you win and lower your bets by one unit when you lose, which at least takes advantage of winning streaks. Unfortunately, if applied to the letter, you don't lower your bets fast enough when you get on a bad losing streak, thereby wiping out your profits.

THE LABOUCHERE SYSTEM OR CANCELLATION SYSTEM

Reportedly invented by Queen Victoria's finance minister, this is one of the most popular methods among serious gamblers. Just be sure to bring your pad and pencil.

First pick a series of numbers, such as 1, 2, and 3. Write those down; each number represents units. You always bet the sum of the two outside numbers. Here the outside numbers are 1 and 3; you add those together and you get 4. So your first bet is four units.

If you lose, you add the amount of your bet to the end of your string of numbers, so now it looks like 1, 2, 3, 4. Your next bet is again the sum of the two outside numbers. Now they are 1 and 4, which gives you a total of five units.

You bet the five units and you win! Now you cross out, or cancel, the two outside numbers you used to bet, in this case 1 and 4. So now you have only 2 and 3. You combine them and you find once again that you're betting five units. You win again and cross out the 2 and the 3. Now you have no numbers, but you do have a profit of $6 (the sum of all your original starting numbers). The big selling point is that you theoretically only have to win one-third of your bets plus 1 to come out ahead, because you cancel two numbers with each win but add only one number with each loss (you did bring a pad and pencil, right?). The downside is that when you do add a number, it's usually a pretty big number. Soon after a bad losing streak, you're betting far more than you can comfortably stomach just to get back to even.

FIBONACCI PROGRESSION

The Fibonacci sequence dates back to the 1100s, and the Fibonacci progression found its way into gambling dens not too much later. The Fibonacci sequence starts with 1, 1, 2, and every additional number is the sum of the previous two numbers: 1, 1, 2, 3, 5, 8, 13, 21, 34, 55, 89, 144, and so on. The Fibonacci system is just like the Martingale except that instead of doubling your bet, you simply follow the Fibonacci sequence with each loss. When you win, you merely bet the previous number to recover your previous losses. You don't

have to be a math nerd to see that if you lose a few hands in a row, you'll be betting enormous sums just to get back to even.

THE PAROLI SYSTEM

This system is the opposite of the Martingale system. You may even hear some gamblers refer to it as the anti-Martingale system. Using this system, you start with one bet and double your bet when you win instead of when you lose.

A plus to using this system is that you don't need a large bankroll. The downside is that you never lock up a profit, and you never know when to stop.

OSCAR'S GRIND

Writer Allan Wilson first described this system in 1965 based on a meeting he had with a gambler named Oscar. With his system for roulette, Oscar reportedly earned a modest but consistent profit.

In the short to medium run, Oscar's grind might, just like any other roulette system, give you a profit if you're lucky. But over the long run, this system will break down like all the others.

It goes like this: You bet one unit on an even-money bet. If you win, there is no sequence, and you keep betting one unit until you lose. After a loss, you continue to bet the same number of units as you just lost. Now when you win, your next bet is one unit larger than your previous bet. When winning, you continue to increase the size of the bet by one unit until you've recovered your losses and have made a one-unit profit. See the example in the table opposite.

Although extremely conservative, the system is surprisingly good and offers a chance to win in the short term with little volatility, as long as you set a maximum limit on how much you're willing to lose in a single spin.

Bet and outcome	Accumulated Loss/Win
Bet 1 unit and lose	-1 unit
Bet 1 unit and lose	-2 units
Bet 1 unit and lose	-3 units
Bet 1 unit and lose	-4 units
Bet 1 unit and win	-3 units
Bet 2 units and win	-1 unit
Bet 2 units and lose	-3 units
Bet 2 units and lose	-5 units
Bet 2 unit and win	-3 units
Bet 3 unit and win	0
Bet 1 unit and win	+1 unit
The series has been won	

Now that you're armed with knowledge and ready to take on the casino, don't assume that the war is already won. Fancy book learnin' is one thing; sneaking past the casino's defenses is quite another.

Sure, you'll go in knowing all you really need to know to win, like whether you should hit that 15 against a dealer's 6. But once you're actually faced with the decision in the heat of battle, with real dollars on the line, remembering the right thing to do will be no small task.

As I said before, the casinos will do everything in their power to get you to abandon your discipline, forget about patience, throw caution to the win, and just gamble. Flashing lights, the loud sounds of winning slot machines, and free-flowing alcohol served by attractive cocktail waitresses all conspire against you. Even your fellow well-intentioned players may steer you wrong with their supposed "superior" knowledge.

And nowadays there's gambling "advice" everywhere you turn, from bookstores to the Internet, even the freakin' Travel Channel. You'll hear plenty of theories, systems, schemes, notions, beliefs, and techniques—some good, most of them B-A-L-O-N-E-Y. So how's a hapless patron able to filter the sound advice from the pie in the sky? Just remember these points:

- **Gambling systems don't work.**

If you discovered how to win consistently from casinos, would you share your secret with the world for a coupla sawbucks? I didn't think so.

- **Remember the five keys to gambling success.**

I've given you the basic tools you need. Whenever faced with a new decision or novel advice, be sure to run it through the keys to see if it fits with what you know to be true.

- **Practice before you pay.**

Before you mortgage your house to fund the next big gambling thing, run the method through its paces, either with a computer simulation or at a low-limit table.

And, to make sure you aren't led astray by all those other supposed gambling gurus, be sure to check out my Web site, www.pitbosssecrets.com, where I answer reader questions, discuss the latest gambling goings-on, and provide the most reliable info around.

In the meantime, may all your hole cards be Aces and all your slot pulls be winners.

GLOSSARY

All-in: To bet the entire amount of chips or money you have in front of you.

Bad beat: When a good hand is beaten by an even better hand. For example, a full house gets beaten by a straight flush.

Basic strategy: In blackjack, the predetermined best set of plays you should make to minimize the house edge.

Betting limits: The minimum and maximum amounts of money you can wager on one bet. You cannot wager less than the minimum or more than the maximum amount posted.

Black: The most common color used for $100 chips.

Bluff: In poker, raising with a weak hand in the hope that other players with better hands will become intimidated and fold.

Board: In poker, the community cards dealt face up in the center of the table are described as "on the board."

Boat: Another term for a full house.

Burn card: The off-the-top card placed on the bottom of the deck or in the discard tray after a shuffle and cut.

Bust: In blackjack, you "bust" if your card ranks total more than 21. If you bust, you lose.

Button: In poker, a small plastic disc used as a marker that is moved from player to player after each hand to designate the dealer position.

Call: In poker, when a player matches the current bet on the table.

Capping: A form of cheating in which a player secretly adds a chip to the top of the bet stack on a winning spot after a decision has already been made.

Card counting: Keeping track of the high and low cards that have been played since the shuffle.

Cashier's cage: The place in a casino where players may redeem their casino chips for cash.

Casino advantage: The edge that the house has over the players.

Check: On most table games, another term for a chip. In poker, if no one else has bet, a player can say "check" to stay in the hand but not bet.

Chips: In general, round tokens used on casino gaming tables instead of cash, though casino personnel call them checks. Technically, "chips" are the round tokens used only at roulette.

Cold: A player or dealer on a losing streak is said to be cold.

Color up: When a player leaving a game exchanges smaller denomination chips for larger denomination chips. For example, exchanging twenty red $5 chips for one black $100 chip (or checks).

Comps: Short for "complimentary." Refers to gifts used by casinos to entice players to stay and gamble, such as free buffets, drinks, and even hotel rooms.

Copy: In pai gow poker, a copy occurs when a player and the banker have the same two-card hand or the same five-card hand. The banker wins all copies.

Croupier: The French word for "dealer," used in baccarat and roulette.

Cut: When the dealer divides a deck into two parts and inverts them after they have been well shuffled.

Cut card: A different solid color card used to cut a deck of cards and to prevent someone from catching a glimpse of the bottom card.

Deal: To dole out the cards during a hand.

Designated dealer: In poker games like Texas hold 'em, the "dealer" gets to bet after everyone else. In a poker room where each game has a resident dealer, a different player serves as the designated "dealer" for each hand.

Deuce: A card with the rank of two.

Discard rack: A rack on the dealer's right side that holds all the cards that have been played or discarded.

Double down: In blackjack, to double your original bet in exchange for receiving only one more card.

Draw: In draw poker, the second round of cards that are dealt.

Drop box: On a gaming table, the box that serves as a repository for cash, markers, and sometimes chips that players have paid the casino in exchange for gaming chips.

Edge: An advantage over an opponent.

Even money: A type of bet that pays you the same amount that you wagered.

Expected win rate: A percentage of the total amount of money wagered that you can expect to win or lose over time.

Face cards: The Jack, Queen, and King of any suit of cards.

Family pot: In poker, when everyone at the table decides to enter a pot.

First base: At the blackjack table, the position on the far left of the dealer that is the first position dealt to.

Flop: In Texas hold 'em, the first three cards dealt face-up in the center of the table.

Flush: In poker, a hand consisting of all cards of one suit.

Fold: In poker, when a player declines a bet and drops out of the hand.

Foul: In pai gow poker, a "foul" occurs when the two-card low hand is set higher than the five-card high hand, or when the hands are set with the wrong number of cards. A fouled hand is an automatic loser.

Four of a kind: Four cards of the same rank, also known as quads.

Full house: In poker, a hand consisting of a three of a kind and a pair.

Green: The most common color used for $25 chips.

Hand: The cards that you hold.

Hit: In blackjack, to take another card.

Hole card(s): In blackjack, the hidden face-down card that the dealer gets. In hold 'em poker, the hidden face-down cards the player gets.

Hot: A player or dealer on a winning streak is said to be "hot."

House edge: The percentage of each bet you make that the house takes in. Winning bets are paid off at less than the true odds to guarantee a profit for the casino.

Inside bets: A roulette bet placed on any number or small combination of numbers.

Inside straight: In poker, four cards of an incomplete straight where the straight can be completed only one way with one card. For example, if a player has the cards Three, Four, Five, and Seven, she needs to get a Six to complete it.

Insurance: In blackjack, a side bet that can be made (up to half your original bet) that the dealer has a blackjack. Insurance is offered only when the dealer's up card is an Ace and only wins if the dealer has a natural.

Joker: The 53rd card in a deck, sometimes used as a wild card.

Kicker: In poker, an odd high card held to settle ties. If two players each have a pair of Aces, the player with the next highest card in hand wins.

Limit: In poker, any game that has a fixed limit for betting or raising.

Loose: Slot machines are loose when they are paying off and giving the house only a small advantage over the player.

Marker: A check that can be written at the gaming tables by a player who has established credit with the casino.

Mini-baccarat: The scaled-down version of baccarat, played with fewer players and dealers and less formality.

Natural: In blackjack, a two-card hand of 21 points. In baccarat, a two-card total of 8 or 9.

Open-ended straight: An incomplete straight that has two ways of being completed. For example, a player holding cards Three, Four, Five, and Six can make a straight by drawing a Two or a Seven.

Outside bets: Roulette bets located on the outside part of the layout, such as red or black, or 1–12. They involve betting 12 to 18 numbers at one time.

Pair: Any two cards that have the same rank.

Pass: To not bet or to fold.

Pat: In blackjack, an unbusted hand worth at least 17 points.

Pay cycle: A theoretical expression that reflects the number of plays required for a slot machine to cycle through all possible winning and nonwinning combos.

Pay line: The line on a slot machine window on which the symbols from each reel must line up. Slot machines can have as many as eight paylines, although most have only one.

Payoff: Your payback; the return you see on a wager.

Payout percentage: Also referred to as the payback percentage, the amount of each dollar played in a video poker or slot machine that the machine is programmed to return to players. Payback percentage is 100 percent minus the house edge.

Payout table: A posting somewhere on the front of a slot machine or video poker machine. The table lists the payouts for all winning combinations.

Pit: An area of a casino in which a group of table games are arranged, where the center area is restricted to dealers and other casino personnel.

Pit boss: The person who supervises all the games and casino personnel associated with a pit during a particular work shift. Pit bosses are in place to watch for cheating, settle disputes, and give comps to big bettors.

Pot: In a poker game, the amount of money accumulated in the middle of the table as each player antes, bets, and raises. The pot goes to the winner.

Pressing: A player is pressing the bet when they let winnings ride by wagering them along with the original bet.

Probability: A branch of mathematics that measures the likelihood that an event will occur.

Progressive: A slot machine whose potential jackpot increases with each coin that is played until it hits. Then it resets to its original number.

Push: A tie hand between a dealer and a player; no money changes hands. A push at blackjack occurs when both the player and the dealer have unbusted hands with the same total points.

Quads: Four of a kind.

Qualifier: In three-card poker, the minimum standard a hand must meet to be eligible to play or to win.

Rack: A plastic container in which you can carry coins or casino checks.

Raise: In poker, a player raises by matching the previous bet and then betting more to increase the stake for the remaining players.

Rake: The money that the casino "charges" for each hand of poker. This is usually either a small percentage or a flat fee taken from the pot during or after the hand.

Rank: The worth of a set of cards.

Red: The most common color used for $5 chips.

Reel: A wheel inside a slot machine window on which the slot machine symbols are printed. The number of reels per slot machine may vary but is usually three.

RFB: Casinos will often comp high rollers free room, food, and beverage.

River: In poker, the final card dealt on the board in a hand of hold 'em.

Royal flush: In poker, an Ace-high straight flush, the best possible hand.

Rush: Being "on a rush" means that you're winning a large proportion of hands.

Session: A series of plays at any gambling game.

Set: In pai gow poker, players "set" their seven cards into two separate hands of two and five cards each. In poker, a "set" is a three of a kind where two of the three cards are in your hand and one is on the board.

Shoe: A plastic or wooden box that holds multiple decks of cards to facilitate dealing.

Showdown: In poker, after the last betting round, the players who remain in the pot must show their hands in the showdown to determine the winner.

Shuffle: Before each hand the dealer mixes up the order of the cards.

Singleton: In poker, a card that is the only one of its rank.

Soft hand: In blackjack, any hand that contains an Ace that can be counted as either 1 or 11 without busting.

Stand: In blackjack, to refrain from taking another card.

Steal: In poker, to win the pot by bluffing.

Stiff: In blackjack, a hand that is not pat and that may bust if hit once. Stiffs include hard 12 through 16.

Straight: In poker, a hand consisting of five cards of consecutive ranks.

Straight flush: In poker, a hand consisting of five cards of consecutive ranks of the same suit.

Surrender: In blackjack, to give up half your bet for the privilege of not playing out a hand.

Third base: In blackjack, the spot nearest the dealer's right hand, which will be played last before the dealer's hand is played.

Three of a kind: Three cards of the same rank.

Toke: A tip given to the dealer in the form of money or chips.

Trey: A three.

Trips: In poker, a form of three of a kind, in which you hold one card and the other two are "on the board."

True odds: The ratio of the number of times one event will occur to the number of times another event will occur. The odds paid in a casino are usually not the true odds.

Turn: In Texas hold 'em, the fourth card the dealers puts on the board.

Two pair: In poker, a hand containing two sets of pairs.

Up card: In a blackjack dealer's hand, the card that is face up for all the players to see before they play their hands.

Vigorish/vig: The fee, or commission, taken by the house.

Wild card: A joker or other card that can be used as any other card to complete your hand.

INDEX

Page numbers in italics indicate charts or illustrations.